CHAPPUIS
MY STORY

CHAPPUIS
MY STORY

by Charyl Chappuis with Paul Murphy

First published in 2024 by Fair Play Publishing

PO Box 4101, Balgowlah Heights, NSW 2093, Australia.

www.fairplaypublishing.com.au

ISBN: 978-1-923236-01-1
ISBN: 978-1-923236-02-8 (ePub)

© Charyl Chappuis and Paul Murphy 2024
The moral rights of the authors have been asserted.

All rights reserved. Except as permitted under the *Australian Copyright Act 1968* (for example, a fair dealing for the purposes of study, research, criticism or review), no part of this book may be reproduced, stored in a retrieval system, communicated or transmitted in any form or by any means without prior written permission from the Publisher.

Design and typesetting by Leslie Priestley.
Photographs from SOPA Images, Alamy, or supplied by Charyl Chappuis via Vachira Kalong (Almonfoto) and Chiraphat Phaungmala (@supersub Thailand).

All inquiries should be made to the Publisher via hello@fairplaypublishing.com.au

A catalogue record of this book is available from the National Library of Australia.

This book is
dedicated to the memory
of my friend Raphael

Contents

The tournament that changed my life	1
How it all began	10
Becoming a world champion — the other tournament that changed my life	18
The big move to Thailand	36
Injury pain — A career put on hold	51
The comeback	61
The move to Muangthong	71
The Port years	84
More than just a game	92
Life after playing	105
Appendix 1: Charyl Chappuis Honours	123
Appendix 2: My best XIs	124
Acknowledgements	125
About the Authors	126

CHAPTER 1

The tournament that changed my life

Adisak Kraisorn had been fouled in the box and I could see that he wanted to take the penalty. But I told him it was mine. I was the designated penalty taker and it was my duty. Adisak and I were roommates at the time, and he just looked at me and said, "You had better score".

December 17, 2014, is a day forever etched in my memory. The ASEAN Football Federation (AFF) Cup may not have the prestige of the FIFA World Cup or the Copa America, but it matters a lot to the 10 Southeast Asian nations who take part. I had been thrust into the spotlight in the first leg of the final as Thailand hosted Malaysia in Bangkok. The second leg would take place in Kuala Lumpur three days later.

The 2014 edition was the 10th time the biannual tournament had taken place and Thailand had history on their side. The War Elephants had won the competition three times to Malaysia's one. But the Thais had gone through a difficult time leading up to this one and Malaysia had been the more recent victors in 2010.

After a cagey 70 minutes, typical of a tournament final, my big moment arrived.

I had been used to taking penalties since I was a kid and it was not usually something that made me nervous. But this one felt different. Thailand hadn't won the AFF Cup in 12 years and I was taking a big responsibility for breaking that sequence in front of about 50,000 expectant fans at Bangkok's Rajamangala Stadium. The weight of a nation was on my shoulders for a very brief moment.

I looked up and saw the clock had gone past the 70-minute mark, so I knew it would be an important goal. As usual, I chose my corner and, fortunately, I hit the ball low to the keeper's right and found the net. My confidence had been so high throughout the tournament and, again, it felt like almost everything was working out well for me. There was relief as I was very conscious that missing the shot at such an important moment could have been the difference between glory and bitter disappointment.

Kroekrit Thaweekarn then scored a second goal to give us a cushion ahead of the second leg, but with a couple of minutes remaining, I missed the opportunity to effectively bury Malaysia and clinch the trophy.

A lot of people looked in awe at the 27-pass sequence that led to my golden chance. They described it as Thailand playing tiki-taka in the style of Barcelona or Spain, but I was mad at myself for not finishing the move with a goal. I really wish I had scored. The move received plenty of attention and more than a million people have seen it on YouTube. How many more would have watched if I had put the ball into the back of the net?

That move represented exactly the kind of team we were. The buildup to the chance was symbolic of the philosophy of our head coach, Zico (Kiatisuk Senamuang). All the movement both on and off the ball showed exactly how we worked as a team.

But I was so disappointed about missing. The ball came to my right foot but I took a little too long to control and shoot, so a defender closed me down. My shot took a slight deflection off him and it missed by a metre to the goalkeeper's left.

At 3–0, it would have been really tough for Malaysia but we left ourselves some work to do and, of course, Malaysia made us work really hard to win the trophy in the second leg.

With just under an hour of the second leg gone, our advantage had been wiped out and the Malaysians led 3–2 on aggregate. Missing that chance looked like it may well come back to haunt me.

Perhaps inexperience had played a part in what looked like our downfall. We were maybe not expecting such an intimidating crowd in Kuala Lumpur. Malaysia had played the semi-final in a smaller venue but moved to the Bukit Jalil Stadium for the final to accommodate a larger crowd. The place was packed with over 90,000 passionate home fans. The size of that crowd just hammers home the importance of the tournament to the population of the region. Not many players have the chance to play in front of so many supporters in their careers, and most of us were only in our early twenties.

My impression was that a number of our team were not quite ready for that kind of crowd and atmosphere. We were nervous, especially in the first half. It didn't help that the referee gifted Malaysia a penalty just six minutes in. It was a shocking decision and if you look back at a recording of the match, my reaction says it all—utter disbelief that he could make such a big decision so early in the game for what was, if anything, a foul on the defender.

But we didn't always help ourselves. Mistakes were made and we went 2–0 down at the end of the first half.

Nevertheless, I could feel that we were gaining in confidence. Although we were disappointed by the half-time score, something special happened during the break.

At first, I was a little bit angry with how the game had been going and I was focusing on myself, but then I noticed a change in the atmosphere. I hadn't been in Thailand long enough to understand a lot of the conversation around me but I could see that our coach, Zico, had taken a phone call. It was a message from the King of Thailand, wishing the team well and saying he believed in us, and he was pushing us to keep fighting to turn things around.

I looked around and many of my teammates looked emotional. It gave me goosebumps.

However, 12 minutes into the second half, we conceded a third goal. While Safiq Rahim's first goal had been a very lucky penalty, his second was a wonderful free kick. Now, we had to overcome the disappointment of going 3–0 down on the night and 3–2 behind on aggregate. It was a really tough moment but I knew that we had 30 minutes left and one goal could change everything. That's exactly what happened.

We had such a winning mentality in the team and it kept us believing. Most of our group had been together since the 2013 Southeast Asian (SEA) Games. Our attitude was always to go out and fight, play with heart and play our style. We knew if we did that, we could beat anyone.

After all, we had proved our quality at the 2014 Asian Games where we beat China and gave South Korea a very hard semi-final and eventually finished in fourth place. I knew that with away goals counting, we still had a chance to lift the trophy, if not win the game.

Zico showed his confidence in us by letting us continue to play in the same style and avoiding any drastic changes despite going into the final 10 minutes a goal behind. When we did finally score, it came from an unlikely source.

I was never known as a goal scorer—not before this tournament and not after it either. My role was more to control the game, dictate the pace of play and help the team play. In this tournament, somehow, I scored a few goals, including two crucial penalties. I had such amazing confidence in front of goal, but that was not my normal style.

When the ball rebounded to me after the keeper saved a free kick, I took it on the half volley with my left foot and didn't even think twice. It was such a special moment for me when it hit the net and I jumped over the advertising hoardings and tried to celebrate with the fans up in their small corner of the stadium.

It was also extremely satisfying to see the reaction of my teammates, coach Zico and the staff. If you score a goal that means a lot, it is an unforgettable moment. As a team, we had not played particularly well in that match. Personally, I didn't think I was having a great game but, of course, one goal changed everything.

The goal gave us one hand on the trophy and then our second goal, a spectacular strike from Chanathip Songkrasin, made sure we were going to win it.

I was proud to be a part of this team and to provide some important goals. Winning the trophy changed my life. But it's fair to say that our success surprised some.

I wouldn't say that the fans and the media expected us to win because, let's be honest, the team was very young. We didn't have some of our strongest players, including Theerathon Bunmathan and Teerasil Dangda. We went more or less with the U23 squad that had been to the Asian Games and added a few older players who were not necessarily starters. But we worked so hard in a training camp before the tournament.

People might expect that working with Zico involves a lot of work with the ball, but it also requires an awful lot of running. That playing style was enjoyable but it was also very hard work.

An inexperienced squad requires a certain type of leader, and Zico is a coach who knows how to deal with young players. He had so many rules. For example, when training started, everyone's shirts had to be tucked into their shorts. If you didn't follow that rule, you had to do 10 push-ups. As a young player, you don't question it, you just do it. But if you tell that to a 35-year-old, the reaction might be different.

The respect for the coach was so high because of everything he had achieved as a player and what he had already achieved with us as a coach. But he was also like a teammate at times because he still got involved in the games at training and in the rondos. He cracked jokes and sang songs and the atmosphere around us was just so positive. We were a real team before, during and after training.

We hung out together, drinking coffee and playing computer games and just had fun. Even on days off, we would get some balls and do a bit of extra work. We wanted to show everyone that we could win the trophy, so both individually and as a team, we were always focused on victory but we took it game by game.

During the buildup and even at our first AFF Cup game, there was almost no Thailand media presence. The country had slipped to an all-time low of 165 in the FIFA rankings just two months earlier, so the apathy was somewhat understandable. In the qualifying rounds for the 2015 AFC Asian Cup, Thailand lost all six matches, including 5-2 defeats to Lebanon at home and away.

Only about 5,000 fans showed up to see the humiliating home match against the Lebanese—the final match in an embarrassing campaign. I spent that match on the bench and was one of just six players in the squad that night who made it to the AFF Cup nine months later. Only one of the starting XI against Lebanon would be selected. It was clear that Zico was aiming for a completely fresh start, unburdened by past failures.

While the younger age groups had been taking positive steps, the senior side still had everything to prove to a sceptical public. But when we beat Singapore and Malaysia in the group stage, more and more people became interested. It was funny to see how fast everything changed.

I had already seen something similar in my career with the Switzerland U-17 side at the 2009 World Cup. We had a media day before the tournament and almost no one was there. When we reached the final, the whole room was full of Swiss media, including TV. It felt a bit like déjà vu in 2014.

Expectations for the AFF Cup may have been low among the media and the fans back home, but the players really believed that we could win it for the first time in 12 years.

The opening match of a tournament is always very important and it can have a big impact on confidence and momentum. The first crucial moment arrived for me in the closing minutes of our first match of the group stage against Singapore.

After training each day, we had been practising penalties and before every game, Zico asked who wanted to take them. I was always the first to raise my hand so it was destined to be my duty.

We had taken an early lead but Singapore soon equalised. It looked like the game was going to end in a stalemate until we were awarded a penalty with just a couple of minutes remaining.

When I got the ball, I wasn't really thinking about the importance of the kick. It was something I had been doing since I was five years old. We may have been playing in Singapore, but there were not that many home fans in the stadium.

I felt a little bit of pressure because I knew that scoring would almost certainly win us the game, but I didn't think about it too much. I chose my corner and managed to put the ball past the goalkeeper, even though he guessed the right way. For me, the hard work had started to pay off.

I ran straight to Andy Schillinger, our physio, because since coming back from the Asian Games I had been struggling with a knee injury and I was so thankful to have him in the national team setup. We had been working on my right knee three times a day —morning, afternoon and evening —to keep the swelling down and allow me to play.

Next up, we had Malaysia at the Jalan Besar Stadium. Our games against them are always competitive and, as they are a neighbouring country, there is definitely a rivalry that adds an edge to fixtures against them.

It had been raining and we were playing on artificial turf, so the ball was moving really fast which was an advantage for us. We controlled the game really well even though Malaysia had a strong side with lots of experienced players.

The Malaysians opened the scoring before I provided an assist for Adisak to equalise for us just before half-time. Malaysia took the lead again in the second half and then I scored a second equaliser. Chanathip got the ball in the box and laid it back to me to hit into the top corner. Fortunately, Adisak scored again to win the game in the final minute and seal our place in the semi-final.

The fact that we had already qualified for the last four meant I was able to sit out the final group match against Myanmar. The coach and the physio made the decision to rest my knee so I would be ready for the two-legged semi-final. With me watching from the sidelines, the boys beat Myanmar 2–0 to keep up the positive momentum ahead of our clash with the Philippines.

At that time, the Philippines were making big strides and were the top country in Southeast Asia according to FIFA rankings. While you have to take those rankings with a pinch of salt, they still suggested the Philippines would be no pushovers.

The first match of the semi in Manila was a really tough, physical battle. Adisak was red-carded, meaning we had to play for much of the second half with 10 men. Our goalkeeper Kawin Thamsatchanan made some good saves and our defence held firm for a 0-0 draw, so we were confident we would finish the job in Bangkok.

We dominated the second leg, winning 3-0 and playing some great football. The Rajamangala Stadium was almost full and the atmosphere was electric. At that point, everyone finally started to believe we had a big chance of winning the trophy. We earned a lot of praise for the style of football we played, always trying to be brave on the ball and playing with passion. It set us up nicely for the triumphant final match and the madness that followed.

Partly because we were such a young group, there were no real superstars or big egos in the squad. However, after winning that tournament, we quickly earned a level of celebrity both on and off the pitch that certainly inflated those egos. There was an open-top bus tour in Bangkok and I didn't really expect us to get as much attention as we did. That kind of thing was reserved for World Cup winners or champions of the European and South American leagues—or so I thought.

We were aware that the country had been behind us when we were playing in Malaysia, but we didn't expect so many fans to show up to celebrate with us on our return home. It was one of the best days of my life and I relished every moment. It was beautiful to see so many happy people on the streets, following us and screaming our names.

This tournament changed the landscape of Thai football for the next few years. From 2015 to 2017, there was a lot of money in the Thai game and a lot of sponsors. Some players got big-money contracts and it was a great time to be involved.

I had already begun to feel my life changing after the Asian Games in 2014. I knew my life was never going to be the same again and the AFF Cup accelerated that feeling. It was exciting and daunting at the same time.

The second leg of the final was played on December 20, so Christmas was just around the corner and I got away from the football fever to return to Switzerland to visit my family and celebrate with them. While it was nice to be back with family and friends after such a great year, there was a downside. Because I was out of Thailand, I missed out on a couple of big opportunities, like TV shows and commercials. The Thai football team was in high demand.

I had an agent in Switzerland who was dealing with the football side of things but I had also employed the services of a Thai agent who helped me with the commercial opportunities that I was starting to receive. At that time, I was just 22 years old and I didn't really know what to expect. It became a bit overwhelming.

Every single day after the final, I was getting several calls a day from my club, Suphanburi, and about 30 calls from my Thai agent. Eventually, I just had to tell them that I was on holiday and I stopped picking up the phone. If I could go back in time, I would have taken time to enjoy the moment more and stayed in Thailand instead of going back to Switzerland, but I just hadn't expected things to become so hectic.

Nevertheless, it ranks as one of the two main highlights of my career. The first was winning the U-17 World Cup with Switzerland. Both tournaments changed my life and had so much positive impact. But both happened when I was very young. It was an incredible journey to get there and it has been a very eventful journey ever since.

CHAPTER 2
How it all began

Since I started living in Thailand, I have become aware of how Switzerland is perceived here. For many people, it is a place they dream about visiting. It is a faraway land of beautiful mountains and lakes, delicious cheese and chocolate. This is the Switzerland of fantasy and the one promoted by the Swiss tourism board. For me, as a kid, it always felt much more mundane.

I was born in Zurich and grew up in Kloten on the outskirts of the city. Compared to the vibrant and sprawling Bangkok, Kloten is a really small town, but I had no concept of that as a child. To me, it seemed like a pretty big place. Kloten is famous for being home to Zurich Airport and for a very successful ice hockey team. Because of this, ice hockey, not football, was the number one sport in the town. But while I loved all kinds of sports, including ice hockey, football was always going to be my focus because that was the direction my dad led me.

From day one, it seemed that my dad lived his passion for the game through me. He had also been a promising football player with St Gallen and Blue Star. Although he never made it to the first team as a professional, he played at a good level.

My childhood years were comfortable as my parents always looked after my interests. As anyone who has followed my career knows, the Swiss side of my nationality comes from my father, while my mum is a native of Chiang Mai in northern Thailand. I also have an older half-sister, Sabrina, who is from my dad's side. She was around more when I was very young, but she is 12 years older. During my childhood, she was at an age where she had other interests. She had to study abroad and went to Australia to visit her mum. I might have had an older brother but he sadly passed away at birth because he was too premature. His name was Charly, so we would have been Charly and Charyl. I effectively grew up as an only child.

My mum and dad separated when I was eight or nine years old and from that age I lived with my dad, not because my mum didn't want me around but because she knew my dad could take care of me and support my interests. A divorce is always difficult for a young child, but it was relatively amicable. My mum understood that being with my dad at such an important stage of my sporting development was better for me even at an early age.

I still saw my mum every week and was also very close to her, but my dad was my coach. We trained so much together in my back garden, and we went to the forest to run. He knew that with extra hard work, you can eventually achieve something. He wasn't in the same league as Earl Woods or Richard Williams, but he was determined to push me to fulfil the potential I showed. And that potential was clear to football scouts from a very young age.

I started to get involved in football at five years old and I played in Kloten for my first three years. When I was eight years old, we played in an indoor tournament in Zurich. I won the player of the tournament and was scouted by Juventus Zurich, which was the city's third professional club after Grasshopper Zurich and FC Zurich.

Having a career in professional football is a long shot regardless of how talented you are and how hard you work, but my dad did his best to boost my chances. He was my inspiration and drove me to training every single day from the age of eight. He was patient enough to watch me train and drive me home afterwards. On some of those cold and wet days, it would surely have been nicer for him to be in a warm home watching TV, but that wasn't his style.

My dad made so many sacrifices for me—standing in the rain in freezing weather, watching me, supporting me and also being my biggest critic. But if life wasn't just about football, it was definitely all about sport. My dad was mad about sport in general and every weekend we used to watch every single sport that was on TV, from skiing to athletics to darts. I also watched football every single day and was a huge fan of Roberto Baggio, Francesco Totti and David Beckham.

Despite developing confidence as a football player, I was a very shy and quiet boy. Sometimes you hear stories about the childhood years of footballers and learn about the mischief they would get up to as young kids. That wasn't my style at all and I wasn't the kind to get into trouble. I think it's fair to say that I tried to get on with everyone. When there were problems, it tended to be because trouble found me on the football pitch. Sometimes, older kids don't like it when another player is better than them and they get a bit mad. If a kid was bigger than me and looked like he wanted to hurt me, I was usually the type to run away and avoid the problem instead of confronting it—I was usually too fast for anyone chasing anyway.

Although I was generally shy in social situations, on the pitch I was a completely different person. When it came to sport, I was usually very good compared to most other kids and I had so much confidence. I was a leader on the field in whatever sport I was playing, including football, basketball, tennis or ice hockey. When you're good at something, you enjoy showing it and I shone on the football field, the basketball court or the tennis court.

I was good at a lot of different sports. I seemed to understand very quickly how the games were played. During the winter, I played a lot of ice hockey because it was so popular in our town. I was a decent tennis player, I was very good at swimming and I was also good at skiing. There was even a time when I had to choose between skiing and football. My dad was a really good skier and I seemed to inherit some of his skills. I entered some competitions and won a few gold medals but once I signed a contract with a football club, I wasn't allowed to ski anymore due to the injury risks. Football was always my number one choice anyway.

But despite my abilities, I was still a little socially awkward. From an early age, I perhaps had a subconscious need to only be around people I could really trust to be my friends. I was never the most outgoing kid but

I found two kindred spirits who operated outside my life as a football player, Rafael and Nick. Like me, Nick was half-Thai and half-Swiss. The three of us were always together as kids. Even now, while I enjoy spending time with my teammates, my closest friends are still people who have nothing to do with football. They work in different fields and I think it helps me to separate my career from my personal life.

At school in the classroom, there were 20 kids and sometimes it seemed like they came from 20 different cultural backgrounds, which can be just like the make-up of a football team. There were Italians, Albanians, Serbians and children with parents from all over the world. This had some positive effects on me as it taught me the importance of respecting diversity from an early age, which would help me a lot later in life.

Occasionally as a teenager, the older kids at school would tease me and my friends. As I was half-Thai, my appearance stood out and I was referred to as Chinese in a cruel way. It was tough at times. At a young age, I felt that being mixed-race created problems for me and I never really wanted to speak about my Thai blood. Of course, now it is totally different and I am proud to be from two countries, but that wasn't how I felt at school.

Partly because of this kind of low-level bullying, I developed the skill of talking my way out of trouble. I wouldn't say I was scared to get into trouble, but I didn't want to disappoint my dad and cause him to worry. If something happened at school, I wouldn't tell him and I would try to figure it out by myself. This wasn't because of a lack of trust. I just didn't want any problems I had to be a burden on someone else.

On the football side, I stayed at Juventus until I was 11 years old and won some big youth tournaments. At that point, I was scouted by Grasshoppers and made the decision to move there. It was a big opportunity as Grasshoppers had been the country's dominant club for the previous decade. Some legends of the Swiss game had played there, including Stephane Chapuisat, Ciriaco Sforza, Kubilay Turkyilmaz and the Yakin brothers, Murat and Hakan.

Some excellent head coaches had also passed through the club. Ottmar

Hitzfeld spent some of his early days with Grasshoppers before going on to become one of the greatest football managers of all time due to his exploits at Borussia Dortmund and Bayern Munich. Leo Beenhakker was not at the same level as Hitzfeld, but he still won several titles at Ajax and Real Madrid before rocking up in Zurich. And then there was Roy Hodgson—former Inter Milan manager and future Liverpool and England boss.

It was quite something to be linked with such a big club as Grasshoppers. Being signed with them meant I was lucky enough to go to a sports school when I got older. From years 1–6, I attended a regular school in Switzerland, but from grades 7 to 9, I went to a sports school in Oerlikon. For the first year, my dad paid the fees by himself and that was quite a sacrifice as it was a very expensive school. However, in the second and third years, Grasshoppers paid my fees as I was representing Switzerland at U15 level by that time.

My dad was really tough and kept me in line during my teenage years. He insisted that I finish school successfully as you never knew what might happen in the future, especially with the possibility of injuries disrupting your progress. It was made clear to me that I had to take my studies seriously to pursue my dream of a career in football. The school was also strict and if you didn't get good results in class, you were not allowed to go to training. From the age of 14, I had 10 training sessions per week and one match, so it was a demanding schedule.

Academically, I was an average student at school, but I was focused and well-behaved. I did my homework on time and didn't try to cheat on exams. I didn't really excel in any academic subjects, but I was pretty good at maths, history and, of course, sports. It can be easy to lose focus on schoolwork when your aim is to become a professional football player, but with the pressure from my parents, I had to maintain my discipline. That was not always easy for a teenage boy and it could be extremely tiring.

My schedule was waking up at 6am before taking the train to practice. We had training from 8am to 9.30am. I had a quick shower, then attended lessons from 10am to midday. Then there was a lunch break and more lessons from 1.30pm to 4pm. I then had more training from 6pm to 8pm and my dad would pick me up to get home by 9pm. I ate dinner, caught up with any homework and went to bed around 10–11pm. That was my normal routine for three years, so I didn't exactly live a conventional life as a teenager.

During my time at the Grasshoppers' Academy, I must have played in all positions. I started as a striker, then I was a number 10. Finally, I became more settled in the position of a defensive midfielder. That really helped me develop my game awareness and as things progressed, recognition from the national team followed.

The first time I was selected for the national youth side, the process began with a list of about 50 players. We were all going to be on trial and this was something I took very seriously. I trained really hard for the trial and did a lot of extra work with my dad. As well as playing a match with the other trialists, there was a test of ball control. We each had to keep the ball up 10 times with our left foot, 10 times with our right, 10 times with both feet, 10 times with our knees and 10 times with our head.

I practised so much to make sure the ball didn't drop and I think I was one of just two kids to manage it during the test. It was another example of my level of focus at that time. I was always determined to show my dad that I could do it and to make him proud.

I was delighted when I was selected for my first official game which took place in Germany in front of a big crowd. We lost, but things turned full circle when we beat them at U-17 level in the World Cup two years later.

After the friendly in Germany, we had several training camps at the Soccer Interaction Academy, which is where many clubs and countries take their players. You live there as a team and many physical tests are conducted on each player. Being in that environment makes you realise you are in a really professional setup.

We all had to do the yo-yo test, the sprint test and jogging tests to make sure our fitness was at the right level. I went there at least a couple of times a year to train hard and do my tests, just to make sure my level was being maintained.

Although I was part of the national team setup, it didn't really change things for me at school. Everyone was aiming for a career in sports, so there was no special treatment. Some of my school mates became professional tennis players, some went to the Olympic Games and a few made ice hockey careers in the NHL (National Hockey League). This helped to keep my feet on the ground as it did not seem a big deal to anyone that I was being recognised by the country—it was normal in our context.

In any case, no one really expected this shy kid from Kloten to become a world champion in the near future. However, all my preparation and hard work would soon pay off.

While my confidence on the pitch was clear, the vice president of Grasshoppers thought I would benefit from taking a trip away from home on my own. Although he and my dad didn't say it at the time, it seemed that this plan was designed to toughen me up.

To qualify for the U-17 World Cup in 2009, we had to compete in the European Championships and finish in the top four. Before the Euros, I had the opportunity to join a 'Lions Club' trip. The purpose was for teenagers to do some volunteer work and gain some life skills. My destination was Finland and the trip would be my first experience of travelling by myself to a different country.

I would be lying if I said I was grateful for the opportunity. I lacked the confidence to take it in my stride as I didn't know what to expect. My English wasn't great and that also made me apprehensive, but the Grasshoppers' vice president had recommended the experience and the trip was free, so it was important that I gained something from it. As it turned out, it would be a really memorable time.

I stayed in Turku with a homestay family for 10 days and then went on a sailboat cruise for six days with lots of other youngsters from the Lions Club. We were put in groups and given different tasks like cooking and cleaning. At other times, we had to help out with sailing duties on deck, sometimes in heavy rain and in cold conditions, stopping off in places to go for a sauna. In the end, I had one of the best experiences of my life. I really opened up and it helped me a lot for the upcoming tournaments.

I came back to Switzerland a different person with more confidence and better language skills. The journey there, on the plane by myself, had been really tough, but I returned as a new man with much better social skills. I went there with no friends and came back with many new ones from Brazil, Turkey, Norway and other countries all over the world.

Fresh from this life-changing trip, I felt great heading to the 2009 European Championships where we were in a group with France, Italy and Spain. The other group had Germany, the Netherlands, Turkey and England. Reaching the semi-finals would clinch a spot at the World Cup and we surprised most people by winning our group before losing our semi-final to a very good Dutch team.

It was a great tournament and I played every minute at centre-back. While I played in a variety of roles at my club, I made the centre-back position my own for the national side.

We could already see the high quality of some of our opponents. Spain had Isco and Koke, Italy had Stephan El Shaarawy, and Germany had Mario Gotze, Shkodran Mustafi and Marc-Andre Ter Stegen. And then there was France, who had so much talent. They had speed and they were bigger than us. We really needed to play an outstanding match to beat them.

Although we lost our semi-final, we had achieved our goal of qualifying for the World Cup and could start preparing for it. There were just a few months between the European Championships and the big one, so we didn't have much time.

CHAPTER 3

Becoming a world champion — the other tournament that changed my life

While I started every game of the European Championship, you can never be sure of what comes next. Of course, I had high hopes of being selected for the World Cup squad, but injuries could have ended my chances and some players who had been in the squad for the Euros did not even get on the plane to Nigeria for the World Cup.

It was time to avoid all unnecessary distractions. I kept my focus, trained hard and avoided socialising in the buildup. I spent pretty much all my time at school, on the football field or at home. I was ready for the tournament and really looking forward to it, and there was no way that I would do anything that might hinder my chances of being in Nigeria.

When the squad was confirmed, I was obviously very happy to see my name confirmed. Nwaknwo Kanu, Ronaldinho and Adriano were some of the standout names that had lifted the U-17 World Cup before going on to have great careers for club and country. In addition to those who had gone home as world champions, countless other big names had played in the tournament. Hidetoshi Nakata and Francesco Totti were there in 1993, Xavi played in the 1997 championship, Michael Essien featured in 1999 and Andres Iniesta's talent was given a wider audience in 2001 before David Silva and Cesc Fabregas made their appearances two years later. In 2007,

Eden Hazard was in a Belgium squad that exited at the group stage, while James Rodriguez failed to score for Colombia, seven years before he ended the 2014 World Cup with the Golden Boot for the top scorer. All these players went on to become household names in world football, highlighting the importance of the opportunity of playing in the tournament.

Equally, the competition's history is littered with players who stood out in their teenage years but failed to make a career in the game. One glance at the squads from past U-17 World Cups suggests that the large majority have relatively modest careers if they manage to progress to the professional game. Like every other player who headed for the World Cup, I wanted this to be a huge step towards becoming a professional football player for the next couple of decades.

As the departure date got closer, it became clear that some non-football-related preparation was required. I had to get a few vaccinations, and I realised there was some anxiety among the parents. I didn't give a lot of thought to the idea of going to Nigeria in particular. As a kid, I was aware of where Nigeria was and I had friends from there. But I didn't know much about what was happening in the country or what to expect when I went there.

We had meetings between the team, the backroom staff and the players' parents. The mums and dads had a lot of questions. The parents were particularly worried about the healthcare in Nigeria and about what would happen if someone got sick or suffered an injury that required emergency surgery. In hindsight, the national side was perfectly prepared for all eventualities, but the concerns were understandable given that Nigeria was a developing country.

When we took the plane to Lagos, there weren't many passengers, so we had plenty of space to sleep and just prepare our minds for the adventure ahead. When we arrived, we had to wait a long time for our luggage and we started to notice that things moved at a slower pace than we were used to in Switzerland. Back home, if you had an appointment, you would be there 10 or 15 minutes before the agreed time. We had moved on to what was popularly known as 'Africa time'.

Once we got out of the airport, we got on our own bus and it has to be said that FIFA did a great job of organising us. The luxury coach had the Switzerland logo on it and it made us feel like we were at a real World Cup. Touches like this are important for young players as it highlights what you have achieved to receive this treatment, while also pushing you to want more of the same.

However, the journey to the hotel was something of an adventure. When I had travelled in Europe, it seemed that any journey from an airport to a destination in the same city would take about 20 minutes. From Lagos Airport to the hotel, it was a 90-minute drive. This was despite having a rather well-armed police escort. There were police in front of us, police by the side of the bus, police behind us and police actually on the bus. They all carried big guns, which was a little scary for a bunch of Swiss teenagers, and you could sense it made some of the staff uncomfortable as well. This was the stuff of movies and not an everyday reality for a group of young lads from Switzerland but, at the same time, it was another eye-opening experience that would stay with us.

The journey may have been long and slightly tense, but when we arrived at the hotel, we quickly felt at home. We were lucky that we didn't have to travel too much for the games as most of them were in Lagos, so we could get comfortable in our new surroundings.

There were certain things we had to be aware of in such an unfamiliar environment, especially drinking water. We weren't simply free to head out and buy some snacks. We had brought all of our own food supplies and were under strict instructions to eat only what we had taken with us.

It was time to get on with preparing for the matches and we had the perfect man in charge. Danny Ryser was a great coach for the Swiss U-17s and an even better person, which is particularly important at the youth levels. Everyone looked up to him, not only when we were on the field, but also in how he prepared us off the pitch and how meticulous he was in looking at our opponents.

We knew we had a mountain to climb in this tournament, but it was always our goal to reach the top of that mountain and win the World Cup. This was not overconfidence, but a very strong sense of self-belief that had been developed by the coaching staff and between the players.

The team spirit had a lot to do with the respect we had for each other. Unlike some other squads, there were no big egos and no one in the team acted like he was better than the others—we were all equal.

Our first game was against Mexico, and our staff did a great job of preparing the team. We dominated that game, though we also needed our goalkeeper to produce a few great saves to keep the Mexicans out. We won 2–0 in the end, and it was fairly comfortable.

The second match was a completely different story. This time, our confidence turned into complacency. Despite the progress of Asian football, the European superiority complex persisted in our group. This was not the fault of our staff as they could sense it. After beating Mexico, we just had an unjustifiable feeling that this would be an easier task.

However, when we were 2–0 down after 20 minutes, we knew we had been mistaken. Japan played some great passing football and we were just overwhelmed by their movement in that opening spell, so much so that we were forced into some tactical changes. Granit Xhaka moved into midfield after starting the match on the wing. This meant that the future Arsenal skipper was playing alongside Pajtim Kasami, another player who would play in the English Premier League.

That change really helped us to assert ourselves in the game. We adopted more direct tactics and started sending long balls up towards our front two of Haris Seferovic and Nassim Ben Khalifa. Our three quick goals either side of half-time transformed the match, and we won 4–3 in the end.

After beating Japan in our second game and sealing qualification for the next round, we were invited to the Swiss Embassy for dinner. This was the only time that we ate outside our own hotel in our time in Nigeria. We were going to break our own rules by eating food prepared by another chef. While it was an invitation that we could not really turn down, it would prove to be a costly dinner. The next day, everyone came down with severe diarrhoea, and the only exercise we did was running to and from the bathroom. This was just two days before we faced Brazil.

Ricardo Rodriguez couldn't play against the Brazilians because he was still too weak after his stomach upset. Everyone lost about three or four kilograms as a result of that meal at the Embassy. What a grim experience it turned out to be. Of course, it would have been difficult to refuse an invitation to our own Embassy, but it could have derailed our tournament.

Despite two days of frequent toilet visits, we had no choice but to prepare for the third group game against the mighty Brazil. They had to beat us to get to the next round. We had already qualified for the last 16 and, from our perspective, winning against the Brazilians would have given us a 90 percent chance of facing Germany in the next round, while losing would probably have led us to meet a weaker opponent.

However, everyone in the team insisted that we should do our best to beat Brazil, regardless of who we would face in the next round. That attitude did not soften in the buildup. We had developed something of a tense rivalry with the Brazilian players as we were staying at the same hotel.

We were aware of the hype around some of their players. We knew that Philippe Coutinho had just signed a big contract with Inter Milan. Of course, we were also aware of Neymar who had already become a star on YouTube.

We saw the Brazilian players a lot around the hotel and there were quite a few exchanges in the lifts. The Swiss squad had quite a few big characters, like Xhaka, Kasami and Seferovic. If they were provoked, they would react and they really wanted to show they would not be intimidated by these players with big reputations.

It was not unusual to be at such close quarters with our opponents at youth level. It had happened several times before, but the relationships between players had been a little warmer. I remember watching Champions League matches with the Spanish squad at a previous tournament. We also had some fun with the Italian players when we stayed at the same hotel in an isolated area.

With Brazil though, it was different. We felt they had an arrogance about them, with Neymar swaggering around and already behaving like the superstar he would become. That made us all the more determined to send them home.

Looking back, it's funny to think about the trash talking we did as we passed each other in the corridor. We couldn't understand their Portuguese and I'm pretty sure they didn't understand Swiss German, but we all understood that we were not saying nice things about each other.

In the end, Neymar had a poor match and was substituted around the hour mark. But Coutinho had a great game. At that time, he was the best player I had ever played against. Ben Khalifa scored an early goal for us and it was then backs to the wall. We rode our luck and nine times out of ten, we would have lost that match. Benjamin Siegrist had to make a number of outstanding saves, but once again we worked really well as a team. By the time we got back to the hotel, Neymar and friends had vacated their rooms and it was time for us to focus on the Germany match.

With the German players, there was nothing like the slightly hostile rivalry we had felt against Brazil. We were more like friends as we shared the same language and had a similar culture. We had also played against them a few times and there was a lot of mutual respect.

It was a special feeling walking out against them in Lagos as I had made my debut against them in very different circumstances. The German national anthem is one of the best and it gave me goosebumps listening to it.

After the World Cup, a DVD was made and I remember it featuring a quote from the coach that went back to that game against Germany two years beforehand. He said that we had been like little kids looking up at our opponents in awe, and this was one of the reasons why we lost that match 4-1. At the World Cup, we had grown enough to look in the eyes of the German players as equals. We had perhaps lacked belief against them before, but not this time.

We were playing against a great team with one of the best players I had ever faced in Gotze. I can't explain why, but I knew from the first minute of that game that we were going to win. Sometimes, you just get gut feelings. Even when they scored a late equaliser to take the match into extra time, I never had any doubts.

Personally, I think I had one of my best games of the competition. I got an assist to set up Rodriguez to open the scoring. Eventually, it went to extra time after a 2–2 draw and, for the second time in the tournament, we won 4–3.

That really made people back home sit up and take notice. Interest had been steadily rising as we made progress through the group stage, but the media really started to arrive after we reached the quarter-finals. You could start to feel the hype. The dream of winning the World Cup was a step closer. You knew that winning the tournament could change your life, and it really became a realistic goal rather than just a dream.

I was happy with the form I had shown even though I was playing at centre-back rather than my usual midfield. Ryser preferred me in that position because I had started there with the U15s. I had played at centre-back for Grasshoppers for a year at U15 level but after that I always played as a midfielder. However, when I was back with the national side, I was always back in central defence.

It certainly had its benefits. If I remember correctly, only Siegrist and I played every minute of every match. If I had played in midfield, I would almost certainly have been rotated or rested at certain points. However, if a centre-back is doing well, coaches tend to avoid tinkering with that position. I was fortunate to have our captain Frederic Veseli alongside me. He had just signed for Manchester City Academy and we made a great duo. Our coach really believed in us.

When we had the ball, it was my job to make the passes that would start our attacks. You could say that I was the smaller, ball-playing centre-back alongside Frederic's more physical approach. I was probably better at reading the game and anticipating where the ball would go. I have always liked to have the game in front of me. Even if I was up against a taller striker, if a long ball was coming towards us, I was good at getting in front of him to steal the ball away.

There was talk that Juventus were asking about me at this time as they apparently thought I had a similar style of play to Fabio Cannavaro. Like the great Italian, I wasn't very tall for a centre-back, but I made up for my limited height with other qualities. I always thought that my style would have been well suited to the Italian game as, growing up, I really admired the likes of Paolo Maldini, Alessandro Nesta and Cannavaro. While I would never be conceited enough to compare myself to these giants of the game, I think there were similarities in our playing styles.

Although I had grown up watching Italian football and developed a great affection for some of their players, I was still determined to send their U-17 team home along with the Brazilians and Germans. Like Germany, we had a good relationship with the Italian side, especially the Italian-speaking Swiss players.

However, the rivalry was intense on the pitch, and we had a really tough match against them. Siegrist had to save a penalty and Veseli was sent off for a last-man challenge when we were 2–1 up. The noise in the stadium was incredible as it was a small venue and there were vuvuzelas blasting all the time. We couldn't hear our coach's instructions after the red card but we managed to work things out by ourselves, changing the system to adapt to playing with 10 men in the final stages.

Our coach told us after the game that he knew we couldn't hear him but we had played exactly as he would have told us to. He was really proud of us and he knew then that we had a real chance of winning the trophy.

Our positive relationship with the Italian squad paid off after we beat them as they replenished our food stocks. Our chef was really grateful as we just hadn't brought enough food. We hadn't expected to go so far into the competition. Italy, on the other hand, were prepared to go the distance. The Italians gave us what remained of their food supplies, so we had some lovely cheeses, tasty pasta sauces and great coffee.

While the matches against Germany and Italy had really pushed us to the limit, the semi-final against Colombia turned out to be surprisingly straightforward, mainly thanks to a game-changing moment in the lucky 13th minute.

Santiago Arias would go on to have a great career playing for PSV and Atletico Madrid, and also featuring for Colombia's senior side at the 2014 and 2018 World Cups. But back in 2009, he had the misfortune to be red-carded after a handball on the goal line. Ben Khalifa scored the resulting penalty and we made the one-man advantage count by going on to win 4–0.

The scoreline maybe flattered us a little. They were fast and gave us some problems on the break. From a personal point of view, the final 30 minutes were difficult as I had received my first yellow card of the tournament and I was anxious about missing the final if I put in a mistimed challenge. I played with some caution and it was lucky we were winning so comfortably.

The match might have been comfortable but the journey back to the hotel wasn't. In fact, we were trapped at the stadium in Lagos as the Nigerian national team's semi-final against Spain was immediately after our match. There was chaos outside the stadium as thousands of people without tickets were trying to get in. Stones and other missiles were being thrown.

Resigned to our fate, at least we had the opportunity to see our hosts and final opponents play as Nigeria brushed Spain aside. We eventually got home and finally had a very late dinner. The following day, we did some recovery work in the pool and packed our bags as we had to fly to Abuja for the final.

Due to our typical Swiss mentality, we arrived very early at the airport and checked in. Then, we sat down and waited and waited and waited... We were on Africa time again.

Our plane did not seem to want to move. We could see our luggage sitting on the tarmac as we sat waiting, uncertain of when we would get moving. Meanwhile, we spotted the Nigerian squad, walking in and walking straight onto their plane.

Our staff were getting nervous but we finally took our flight and arrived in Abuja several hours later than planned. We checked into the hotel, got to our rooms and our bags were not waiting for us. It was frustrating, but we kept our cool. All our baggage finally arrived; it just took more time than usual. We had a late night but we still had two more days to prepare. The way we were treated just gave us more motivation.

We knew Nigeria would be very tough opponents, but we also knew that their preparations had been disrupted by FIFA's new age checks. MRI wrist scans were used to check that players were not over age and Nigeria had to completely overhaul their squad in the buildup. This was probably one of the main reasons why they went 3–0 down during their first match against Germany, though they recovered to draw 3–3.

Although I was about to play the biggest game of my life, I didn't feel too much pressure. I just prepared the same as usual. I have particular habits in terms of when I eat. I like evening games because they allow me to take an afternoon nap. I just did my own thing while fitting into the training and meeting schedules. I watched one of my favourite films, *Remember the Titans*, as it motivates me a lot. Denzel Washington's role as an inspirational American football coach is uplifting and inspiration was what was needed before such a huge match.

The coach played a video at our pre-match meetings that included all the goals we had scored in our time together. After each game, the video got longer. The soundtrack to the video was the Abba song, *The Winner Takes it All*. We didn't know at the time that the lyrics to the song were about divorce, so the message conveyed by the title worked for us. Every time we saw that video, we got goosebumps and went straight to the bus to get ready for the game.

Ahead of the final, there was a slight issue between two of our players but it was really well handled. Seferovic and Ben Khalifa were both in with a chance of winning the Top Scorer award as both were on four goals. I think Seferovic was unhappy because he had been lining up at the back post for corners and he felt he should have been getting more opportunities. During the tournament, every time the ball reached Ben Khalifa, it seemed he wasn't making the right contact on the ball and it never reached Seferovic.

But our assistant coach had scouted Nigeria and one thing he had noted was that they didn't defend the back post very well. He told Seferovic to trust him. He insisted he should stay at the back post in the final and that he would get his chance. As it happened, it was Seferovic's back-post header that won us the World Cup.

We played in front of 66,000 passionate home fans. It was loud and there were lots of vuvuzelas, but we managed to shut that out when we were on the field. Nigeria was bigger, faster and stronger than us, and especially dangerous on the counterattack. But we had an amazing game plan.

The final stages of the match went so slowly. We just wanted to hear the whistle. When the referee finally blew full-time, I sat down by myself as it dawned on me that I was a world champion. There were wild celebrations on the field and when we received the trophy, we all had our names on the front of our shirts. This was to do with money.

We started the tournament playing to win the title and achieve something great. However, as we progressed in the tournament, some players wanted more recognition and, of course, we spoke to players from other countries. They were being promised big bonuses, but we had no financial incentives. For me, winning the trophy was much more important than any bonuses, but not everyone was happy with the situation. Showing our names on the front of our shirts was a way of expressing how important we felt as individuals and to earn more recognition for what we had done.

As usual, after winning a big competition, there was a lot of singing and dancing. I was interviewed by a Swiss TV channel on the pitch and apparently up to two million people in Switzerland were watching, which was a huge audience for such a small country. It was crazy to think that almost a quarter of the whole nation was watching us.

In the lead-up to the match, our hotel staff had been teasing us about how Nigeria were going to beat us comfortably in the final. But they were very magnanimous in defeat, and when we got back to the hotel, they joined in the celebrations.

We had dinner and I remember our fellow Swiss Sepp Blatter, FIFA President at the time, was there. He gave a speech expressing his pride at finally being able to award a trophy to a Swiss team. It was a great evening, but I was also exhausted after such a long tournament. Some people partied long into the night but at one point I just wanted to be back in my room and reflecting on the moment in my own way.

Unfortunately, we didn't have FaceTime or Zoom in those days, but I sent my dad a long message to acknowledge that without him, I wouldn't be where I was—a world champion. I wanted to thank him for all those times he had taken me training in the forest on some grim, rainy days, and all the time he had taken to drive me to games and training, not to mention his financial support.

We flew home the next day and thousands of people were there to welcome us. Many were family and friends, but there were also a lot of fans and media. We got the red-carpet treatment as we walked out with the trophy and everyone cheered us. We also had a stage set up and had to give some speeches. Then the players who were from Zurich were invited to the city hall for a reception where we gave more speeches and received some gifts.

Despite all the hype, most of us were just happy to be home again with our families after such a long time away. We only had a couple of days' rest before going back to our clubs.

It had been an incredible few days, but it was also challenging to grasp that everything had changed for me. It was sometimes difficult to know how to deal with the sudden attention. Everyone wanted to pat me on the shoulder, saying how good I was. They wanted to invite me to go out partying and get everything for free. Later, the same thing would happen in Thailand after the 2014 AFF Cup. Out of nowhere, lots of football players wanted to be my friend.

At the age of 17, it was a lot to take in. I didn't have an agent at that time and I was getting a lot of calls and so was my dad. Grasshopper wanted me to sign a new professional contract, and other clubs were also looking to sign me as a result of my performances at the World Cup.

The rumoured interest from Juventus turned out to be real, and I had a big decision to make. It was incredibly flattering to be courted by one of the biggest clubs in the world. Juve was the club of legends like Roberto Baggio, Pavel Nedved and Zinedine Zidane. Alessandro Del Piero was still there after 16 years and, at that time, the dressing room would also house World Cup winners like Gianluigi Buffon, Fabio Grosso and David Trezeguet. From a distance, it must have looked like a straightforward decision but it wasn't at all. Inside, it didn't feel right. I didn't think I was ready and I turned them down.

Juventus were not used to being rejected and it was unusual for them to give someone a second chance, but that's exactly what happened. Gianluca Pessotto, a stalwart of the club and Champions League winner in 1996, decided to take matters into his own hands. He was their youth team coach at the time and he drove all the way to Switzerland to meet me. I vividly remember sitting in front of him and being told that the opportunity to move to Juventus only comes around once in a lifetime. And here I was being given a second chance.

Looking back now, it might seem ridiculous and somewhat crazy that I said no for a second time, but I remember that the opportunity just seemed to come too quickly in the aftermath of all the hype around our U-17 World Cup win. I can't clearly explain why I said no, it was just a feeling I had. I was a very shy person off the pitch and not ready to leave home, learn a new language and adapt to a new culture in the spotlight of one of the most famous football clubs on the planet.

There was also the fact that I had been indoctrinated with the Swiss mentality that encourages players to prove themselves in Switzerland first before they move abroad. It seemed to be the sensible thing to stay at Grasshoppers and develop my career there. Many players have rushed into moves to big clubs and ended up sliding into obscurity and maybe even failing to have a career in football.

However, it may not have done my career any harm to have had a spell at

Juventus on my CV. Even if things didn't work out, I would still have been able to return to Switzerland as a player who had been signed by Juventus. I'm not sure if that would have helped my career in the longer term, but it might have opened some more doors.

Perhaps it was a mistake to sign my first big contract without an agent. With one, I might have been able to work something out with Juventus to ensure there was a clause in my contract allowing me to go somewhere on loan if I could not get regular game time. For me, the important thing between the ages of 18 and 21 is to play and develop. It does not help to be warming the bench or left out of the squad, no matter which club you play for.

I made a decision and it's one I have to live with. When I told friends and family that I had rejected an offer from Juventus, they told me I was crazy but that was an easy conclusion from their perspective. I still saw myself as a very young player with a lot to learn, but just from being a World Cup winner, my market value had shot up to one million Euros. It just felt that it was only a matter of time before more big clubs came for me, and perhaps by then I would be physically and mentally ready for the move.

I never really look back and wish I had taken that offer. It's not my style to have regrets and it's just part of the journey of being a footballer. In the end, I stayed where I was. My dad helped with the new contract negotiations and ultimately, I signed for four years at Grasshoppers.

It wasn't long until another club approached me. Just a few months later, SV Hamburg expressed an interest in signing me and, again, it got as far as a meeting with their representatives. The president of Grasshoppers agreed to let me go to Germany for a fee of $US 1million. This time, the deal felt right. It was another very big club with a rich history, but not at the same level as Juventus. It felt like a more comfortable step to make both on and off the field. While the city on the Baltic Sea was a considerable distance from Kloten, I would have few issues with the language and culture. Hamburg did not have the same glamour as the Italians but they still had a number of stars in the dressing room. Ruud Van Nistelrooy,

Jerome Boateng and Marcus Berg were some of the more recognisable names that I would have rubbed shoulders with had I signed.

I agreed to everything in the contract, but Hamburg then had a change of sporting director and they pulled the plug on the deal. It was disappointing but I remained philosophical. These things happened in football and I was confident that another big club would come calling.

I was still a school student at this time but after winning the World Cup, the school helped me a lot. I had already taken most of the necessary tests and was given an easier schedule to allow me more time to focus on football. Every morning, I had training with the first team, and I spent afternoons at home either studying or at school. I also had my first girlfriend around this time.

Looking back now, having won the U-17 World Cup and then joining the first team setup at Grasshoppers, maybe I thought I had made it. Until that point, something that had always given me the edge in my career was that I worked harder than others. I used to go running in the forest, and I worked on my shooting technique with both feet.

But at the age of 17 or 18, your head is easily turned. Many people are giving you compliments after a World Cup win and you know that teams like Juventus and Hamburg SV are interested in you. And, at this point, I stopped listening to my dad as much as I used to.

He told me that just training for two hours in the morning wasn't enough. He still wanted to work with me to do extra practice or training in the afternoon. Unfortunately, I didn't listen. After all the sacrifices of my early teenage years, I just wanted to enjoy my free time more, either watching movies or hanging out with my girlfriend. It was definitely a mistake to lose my focus like that.

Another thing I remember was my first training session with the Grasshoppers first team. I was so motivated and eager to impress that I was running around and launching into sliding tackles. I really wanted to show everyone that I was good enough both physically and mentally. But after that session, club captain Vero Salatic took me aside and told me that in first-team training, we didn't do sliding tackles. Of course, I listened but then a month later, head coach Ciriaco Sforza called me into his office and suggested that I didn't look like I was trying hard enough at training. It was a confusing message.

Perhaps I had paid too much attention to what Salatic said and it affected the way I approached training and inhibited me somewhat. It did seem like I hadn't made a positive first impression and that was disappointing.

Even though I was still very young, it seemed to me that the best thing for my career would be to get out and play regularly and it felt like I would have to wait for my chance at Grasshoppers. I had been in their setup for almost 10 years, and I really felt ready to play as a professional. It seemed that it might be better to go somewhere I was really wanted. If a club buys you, they invest in you and give you an opportunity to prove yourself. I had been around Grasshoppers for so long, and perhaps there was less patience elsewhere.

It was also a little frustrating to see Xhaka move into first-team football ahead of me. Two Grasshoppers teammates and I had signed our first professional contracts six months before him. I had been on the bench for Grasshoppers against Basel when Xhaka was still in the stands. But Xhaka soon had a coach who had faith in him and he became a first-team regular for Basel while I was no further advanced.

I was on the bench for the first team quite a lot and I played in cup games but never in the league. If the U23 team had weekend games, I played with them. Perhaps I was too impatient and should have understood the need to bide my time and fight my way into the first team's starting XI, but I just felt frustration.

My frustration would get worse when I was on duty for the Swiss U19 side and I suffered a clean break to the metatarsal bone on the outside of my foot. The injury required surgery and kept me out for four months, but I recovered just in time for pre-season ahead of the 2011–12 league campaign.

During my period out of action, I naturally fell further from the first-team picture at Grasshoppers, so it seemed a good idea when Locarno offered to take me on loan for the new season. Locarno is a beautiful little town in the Italian-speaking part of Switzerland and FC Locarno was a small club one level below the top tier. But coach Davide Morandi really wanted to take me there and pushed really hard because knew me well from my time in academy football.

That season, there was a change in the structure of Swiss football as they wanted to reduce the number of teams in the second tier. It meant five teams would be relegated that season. FC Locarno were among the favourites for the drop, but it turned out to be an amazing season.

I played in every match and we eventually finished in ninth spot, 11 points clear of the relegation zone. Because I was so involved and we played some great football and surprised many people, it was one of my most enjoyable seasons.

On a personal level, it was the first time I had lived away from home, so I learned a lot about myself. I worked really hard and had a great relationship with the coach, so it proved I still had the discipline of my youth. My confidence really returned after the injury had disrupted my development. I returned to Grasshoppers, hoping that the experience would improve my chances of making the breakthrough back at my hometown club. That hope was higher because there had been a change of head coach with Uli Forte replacing Sforza.

When I started pre-season training at the club, the 2012 Olympic Games were taking place at the time. A few players from Grasshoppers were in the Swiss squad, so I thought that might improve my chances of some game time.

However, I had received an offer from Lugano for another loan deal in the second tier. Morandi had moved there from Locarno and wanted to work with me again. As Lugano was a bigger club than Locarno, the move was appealing even if it meant playing in a lower division again. At 20 years old, it was really important not to spend a season on the bench, so I had a very frank conversation with Uli Forte about my situation at Grasshoppers.

Forte suggested I would get some game time while certain players were at the Olympics but warned that it would be more difficult when they returned to Switzerland. After weighing up my options, I decided to go to Lugano as it seemed certain I would be playing every week and because I knew the coach so well.

The first five or six games at Lugano were great. We started the season in good form and were top of the table. But somehow the wheels came off and Morandi was fired after a few defeats. This changed the atmosphere around the club and I was lucky that Buriram United came for me at the right time.

I had gone to Locarno and then Lugano to develop my football career and improve my chances of making the breakthrough at Grasshoppers or earning a move to another European club. From a life experience point of view, I learned a lot about Swiss-Italian culture and food. It also became clear that the people were very different from the German part of the country. During summer, it was one of the most beautiful places I had ever seen. However, it did not take me closer to my footballing goals.

My time in Swiss football would soon be over, and an unexpected and exciting new chapter was about to begin. My mother's homeland was calling.

CHAPTER 4

The big move to Thailand

Before my move to Locarno, I had taken on an agent, Rolf Muller. Given it was the final year of my contract at Grasshoppers, he was looking at different options and Buriram United was just one of them.

Although it didn't strike me as a particularly appealing option at the time, Rolf was very supportive about me moving to Thailand. He said we should listen to what they had to say and that I should keep my options open.

I had actually been on Buriram's radar for a few years. They had been monitoring my progress because they were aware of this half-Thai kid who had won a World Cup but when they initially made contact a couple of years earlier, I didn't really have much interest. Of course, things didn't quite work out as I had hoped in the years that followed and I am glad they persisted with trying to persuade me to make the move to Thailand.

Buriram were still showing a lot of interest while I was at Lugano and their representative, Tadthep Pitakpoolsin, flew from Thailand to visit us for a day. This really made an impression as getting from Thailand to Lugano is not a straightforward journey. It really demonstrated how much the club wanted me.

We had an interesting chat that gave me a lot to consider, but I wasn't completely convinced. I still had dreams of a career in Europe and felt that I could still make it at Grasshoppers. Having won a World Cup, I had bigger dreams than a move to the Thai League.

However, I was still intrigued by the opportunity, and the next step was to visit Thailand with Rolf for a couple of days just before Christmas 2012. I had been there on holiday several times as a kid but it had been about 10 years since my last trip, so I didn't remember that much about it. On previous visits, I had spent most of my time in Chiang Mai where my mother's family comes from.

Buriram booked us on a business class flight to Thailand—my first opportunity to make the step up from economy. We were picked up at the airport and taken to stay in a nice hotel in Bangkok, so they were doing a very good job of selling the club to me. A bit of luxury always makes a positive impression.

We drove to Buriram and saw the stadium. It was brand new at the time and really impressive. The people at the club were very welcoming and I was also introduced to Mr Newin Chidchob, the club president.

They did their best to make me feel at home because they knew it was a huge decision for me to make just before my 21st birthday. I was still very young for a person who is close to his family and likes to be around them.

When we had dinner, Tadthep told me he was sure I would be a big hit in Thailand, not just on the pitch but off it as well. And then there was the contract offer. Just like other parts of the club, it really exceeded my expectations and it was a deal that I just couldn't turn down. It was a much better contract than the one I had with Grasshoppers at the time. Because I had signed that deal without an agent, perhaps the club had taken advantage of me a little. Of course, if things had turned out differently with SV Hamburg or Juventus, I would have been in a different league financially. But, in the circumstances, the offer from Buriram was a dream.

Growing up in Europe, you hear nothing about Thai football and little about Asian football in general. But my time in Buriram had really altered my perspective. This was a club that had a purpose-built stadium to hold more than 30,000 spectators and excellent training facilities. Another impressive detail was that the players already had GPS trackers for data analysis. This may have been a relatively remote area from a European perspective, but it was no footballing backwater.

Robbie Fowler had played in the Thai League just a couple of years beforehand, so he had obviously been convinced that it had enough credibility for someone who was a Liverpool legend. At the other end of the scale, I was made aware that Frank Acheampong had joined Buriram at just 17 years old. The Ghanaian impressed so much in the Thai League and the AFC Champions League (ACL) that Anderlecht took him to Belgium for a fee of around one million Euros.

This convinced me that it would not be a dead-end career move. I would be joining a fairly young league that had a record of attracting some top talents at both ends of their careers. The last thing I wanted was to go to a league with a poorer standard and see my career stagnate. There was so much that I still wanted to achieve and Buriram seemed to offer a suitable platform to continue my development.

I returned from Thailand to talk things over with my family and my girlfriend at that time. Ultimately, I made the decision to sign for Buriram as the offer would allow me to support my mum and I knew I would also be able to help my dad out financially. It had always been my goal to support both of them and this contract allowed me to do that. My mum even moved back to Thailand eventually.

After that, everything seemed to pass very quickly as there were so many things to do in a short time. Top of the list was becoming a Thai citizen. My mum had to prepare all the paperwork to allow me to apply for Thai citizenship and the passport and ID card that comes with it. This had to be done in a hurry to make sure I was eligible to play in the ACL as a Thai player and not as one of the foreign quotas. The tournament had limits on players from overseas, so Buriram wanted to fully utilise their existing quota.

The club had an ACL playoff against Brisbane Roar at the beginning of February, and they were really pushing me to be ready for that. It was a huge match for Buriram, so they wanted to have the strongest possible squad.

I arrived in Thailand on January 9, 2013, three days before my 21st birthday. If things had been hectic before my departure, they were just as hectic when I arrived in the country that would become home.

The first priority was to pass my medical in Bangkok. It was a very thorough examination and took six hours—another indication of the club's professional approach. From there, I was driven to Buriram and even though it was 2am when I arrived, I went straight to the team camp rather than a hotel.

The first teammate I met was Chitchanok Xaysensourinthone, a fellow Swiss-Thai who was already at the club. It was nice of the club to have him greet me as it again showed their attention to detail in helping me to settle quickly.

Chitchanok and I became roommates for a while but, despite sharing the same nationality, we did not share the same language. He came from the French part of Switzerland and couldn't really speak much English or German. My French was very limited, so we mainly communicated in a mixture of broken Italian and Thai. We have been close friends ever since.

When people in other countries think about Thailand, the image tends to be of temples, beautiful beaches and the hustle and bustle of Bangkok, but Buriram doesn't really fit into that picture. Although the city has developed considerably over the years, it still had limited facilities when I arrived. But I didn't have to worry about accommodation because communal living was required.

In my time at the club, there was a rule that everyone had to stay in the team camp during the three days before a game. In 2013, we had two matches almost every week of the year because we won both domestic cup competitions and also had a very good run to the quarter-finals of the ACL.

I decided to just stay in the camp and for the first couple of months, I stayed with Chitchanok. For the rest of the year, I was with Theerathon Bunmathan. It was strange to spend a whole year without a permanent home. I was either in the camp or in a hotel and there were lots of flights both within Thailand and across Asia. For a 21-year-old living in a new country, far from his family, loneliness was a real possibility, but I was hardly ever alone. There was no time to think too much. The routine was to wake up, train, have lunch, rest, train, have dinner, watch a movie, and go to bed.

It was good for me just to be able to focus on my football.

Of course, at times it felt tough to have such little free time at that age, but the methods were justified by our results on the pitch that year. The club did everything they could to create a winning culture with their facilities and the way they looked after the players. It is no accident that Buriram have become the most successful team in the country.

On the football front, I really had a baptism of fire. My debut was in the ACL playoff, which was a one-off match to decide who reached the group stages. Brisbane Roar were supposed to host the match but a scheduling clash meant the tie was switched to Buriram and we certainly took advantage.

Even though we were at home, it was still considered an upset that we won on penalties after a 0-0 draw. It was great for me to score my penalty in the shootout and make an early contribution to what was to be a thrilling run to the last eight.

My second match was another big one, facing Buriram's biggest foes — Muangthong United. Although the two clubs had only been in existence in their modern forms for a few years, an increasingly bitter rivalry was building as they fought for domestic supremacy.

My first experience of this match-up came in the Kor Royal Cup—the curtain-raiser for the new season and an opportunity to lift a trophy. We won 2-0 to continue a very positive start to the year.

There were a number of memorable moments for me in the months that followed, including scoring my first goal directly from a corner against Suphanburi. I also received my first call-up for the Thailand national team but, unfortunately, I could not play as the necessary paperwork could not be completed in time.

Frequent changes of head coach are a feature of Thai football and Buriram was no exception that season. When I arrived, Attaphol Buspakom, more commonly known as Coach Tak, was in charge and he was, along with Zico, the best Thai coach I have ever worked with. Tragically, he passed away at a young age just a couple of years later. When coach Tak moved to Bangkok Glass in May 2013, Englishman Scott Cooper took over. Under Scott, we defended really well and did a lot of work on set pieces. But he lasted just a few months before Spain's Alejandro Menendez arrived in September.

Despite the changes, we remained dominant domestically. We were in such ruthless form that we were no longer talking about winning, we were talking about how many goals we would win by. Everyone was pulling in the same direction and there was such a hunger within the group.

The team had a strong Spanish flavour that year as it included Carmelo Gonzalez, Osmar Ibanez and Javier Patino. We were particularly lucky to have Osmar at centre-back as he is probably the best foreign player I have played with in the Thai League. It wasn't just his quality but also his mentality. He was one of those players who, in a tight game, could make the difference between winning and losing.

I played in almost every match of the ACL campaign and scored against China's Jiangsu Sainty, but that goal, while vital to the team sealing a 2–0 victory, would prove costly. My goal came on a breakaway and as I ran to the fans to celebrate, I leapt in the air. I must have jumped a thousand times in my life without suffering any physical injuries, but this time my landing was awkward and I jarred my right knee as I overstretched.

After a scan of my knee, we decided against surgery but it still took two months for me to return to action, and I missed the ACL's last-16 tie against Bunyodkor from Uzbekistan.

It was good to be back in time for the quarter-final against Esteghlal from Iran and what would turn out to be another amazing experience. The away match in Esteghlal was played in one of the most impressive atmospheres of my career to date and really highlighted just how passionate fans in the ACL could be. The stadium was full, and the attendance was approaching 100,000, but it was a men-only affair, with the exception of Newin's wife, Karuna.

We played pretty well in that match, but we conceded early when what seemed to be intended as a cross landed in the goal. We managed to keep things tight after that and, returning to Thailand just 1-0 behind made us confident we could turn things around. Osmar gave us the lead in the second leg, but the Iranian side stepped up a level in the second half of the match and eventually won 2–1.

The ACL was a great experience, especially the group stage as we held our own against teams like FC Seoul. We definitely put Thai League football on the map.

All in all, it was a wonderful year for me both on and off the field. I developed a much better understanding of Thai culture and the people. Sleeping in a camp in a shared room three days before every game may sound difficult from the outside, but when you're winning every game, it's so much easier because morale is so high. Things never became strained within the group because we developed such a strong team unit and ended the season unbeaten in domestic football.

Some thought that life in Buriram might be challenging but there was a surprisingly high number of foreign residents, and some had opened their own restaurants, so food was never a problem. I was already used to Thai food but if I missed anything in particular, it was easy enough to find it. On our occasional days off, I enjoyed going to Bangkok and spending a bit of money as you didn't get many chances to buy stuff in Buriram.

However, it was an exciting time to be in Buriram as the city was at an interesting stage in its development. The motorsport racetrack was being built and several new hotels were being constructed, so it really felt like we were part of something significant, not just for the football fans but the whole area.

Playing for Buriram was not the only highlight of the year as I also got to face some of the biggest names in world football. I was selected for a Thailand XI to face Liverpool and then Barcelona when Europe's top clubs came to town. It was particularly special to face Barcelona as they had always been my favourite team.

Unfortunately, the timing of the match wasn't great as it came just after my return from my knee injury and I was still struggling to get up to speed. The Barca of 2013 was not the team you wanted to play when you were not at the top of your game. I was knackered after 10 minutes, chasing the ball as Barcelona passed it around with ease.

It was a bit of a dream come true to be playing against what was considered the best team in the world at that time. I also had the opportunity to play against one of my biggest idols—Cesc Fabregas. Adding to the sense of occasion was the fact that Neymar scored his first Barcelona goal in the game, having recently been signed from Santos. Of course, this wasn't the first time our paths had crossed as I had faced him in the 2009 U-17 World Cup. In that game four years previously, he had played well below his potential. By 2013, he was one of the biggest names in world football.

There was quite a contrast playing against Liverpool. The English side were bigger and physically stronger and it felt like they were on a different level from that point of view. But then we played Barcelona and we were up against several players who were smaller and didn't look very physically imposing. In addition to Neymar and Fabregas, they had Lionel Messi and Pedro. None of these guys were big, but their talent always more than made up for any lack of physicality.

Playing against Barcelona, it felt like they were 10 steps ahead of us. The strange thing was that they made the game look so easy, it felt like I would not be out of place playing with them. Of course, I am not suggesting that I could have played for them, they just made me feel that way. I loved the kind of football they played back then—truly the beautiful game. On the other hand, against Liverpool, I was made to feel that I would have been well out of my depth in that side because of their physicality.

Barcelona ended up beating us 7-1. It would have been nice to have kept the score down a little, but you had to just appreciate the experience of being on the pitch with those players and seeing what made them so good at close quarters. I knew them from watching them on TV all the time, but it was a completely different experience to play against them. I wasn't disappointed to lose 7-1, I just appreciated the opportunity to share the pitch with a side that has gone down in history as one of the best of all time.

It shouldn't be forgotten that Zico was coaching us at the time, so we didn't park the bus. We wanted to give a show for the fans and have a go at Barcelona. It was a friendly game, so there was little point trying to set up and stop our opponents. We tried to play football and ended up suffering a heavy defeat.

There were some ups and downs that year and the injury was obviously a low point, but I had many winners' medals in my pocket. There was an opportunity for one more when I was called up for the Thailand squad for the 2013 South East Asian (SEA) Games.

Some people might have expected making the switch from Switzerland to Thailand to be a difficult one. Just four years earlier, I had been world champion with the country of my birth and upbringing. At just 21 years old, it may have seemed too early in my career to accept that I was unlikely to be good enough to become a full international for the Swiss side.

However, representing Thailand didn't require much thought. It was yet another welcome reward for my form in a successful first year. Everything was happening so quickly at the time that it just seemed a logical step rather than an emotional decision. Having moved to Thailand, I knew it would be very difficult for me to play for the Swiss national team, so I didn't want to miss out on the opportunity.

Earlier in the year, I had already been called up for Thailand's senior side for an Asian Cup qualifier in Lebanon. I actually joined the squad and trained with them on that occasion but my paperwork was incomplete so I wasn't eligible to play. It was still an important experience for me as I got to know many of the players who would become my teammates.

The welcome I received from the squad was very encouraging despite the fact that I had only recently arrived in Thailand and couldn't speak much of the language. Jakkapan Pornsai helped me a lot because he spoke decent English and, of course, there was some banter, but it was mainly directed at my growing reputation as a 'handsome' football idol. Some players suggested that people shouldn't stand next to me when photos were taken as it would make them look ugly, while others suggested they should get their photos taken with me to raise their own profiles. It was all good-natured stuff and helped me to integrate.

I did my best to practise and improve my Thai. Being immersed in the language helped me a lot. At the time, I was the only half-Thai in the squad, but it wasn't something that I dwelled on. I was treated very well. However, in the future, perhaps this attitude towards half-Thai players changed somewhat as more and more started playing in Thailand and were selected for the national side. Perhaps the local players felt that their places were under threat and it was not fair for guys to come from abroad and almost immediately get a call-up for their adopted country. That said, I never felt any personal hostility because of my background.

And, of course, it was recognised that my mum was from Thailand and that always gave me an attachment to the country. When I was selected for the U23 squad, I had no hesitation accepting as it was an honour and represented my future. All my years playing for the youth teams of Switzerland had been great, but they were now part of my past.

Of course, I spoke with my dad about it and he understood it was the right decision. It was all about me committing to this new chapter in Thailand. I never saw it as a short-term move.

The SEA Games featured the U23 squads from participating nations and Thailand were the most dominant force in the football competition's history. However, we had missed out on medals at the previous two tournaments so there was pressure to ensure this didn't happen for the third time in a row even though the event has a fairly low profile on the international stage.

I had already spent a fair bit of time with the U23 squad as we met several times for camps during the year. One issue was that Buriram and the Football Association of Thailand did not have the best relationship at the time and the club was reluctant to release players for international duty. However, I was selected for the SEA Games and went to Myanmar along with Theerathon and Adisak.

I didn't start the first match against Timor Leste but started every one afterwards. The core of the SEA Games squad was the team that would lift the AFF Cup one year later. Players like Chanathip and Narubadin

Weerawatnodom still weren't regular starters because of their age, but they really benefited from the experience and have gone on to have great careers.

In the second match of the group stage, we were up against the host nation and the stadium was packed. The streets of Yangon were also full of local fans and the vibrant, carnival atmosphere reminded me a lot of Nigeria. The final was somewhat different as we won against Indonesia in Naypyidaw. The new capital of Myanmar felt like a ghost town compared with Yangon and the crowd was very small.

But it was a great way to end the year as it meant another medal and another trophy. It was also a very important step for the national side as such wins breed confidence and that would soon pay dividends at senior level.

The year went by really fast and it was obviously a lot of fun because we were in the habit of winning. However, I was really looking forward to going home to visit my family at Christmas. Once the SEA Games were done, I flew to Switzerland but only had two to three days at home. I had to come back before New Year as Buriram insisted on celebrating with the team. They organise a big party every year.

The Buriram way is clearly a successful model and it can be justified by the club's achievements. However, it was also quite draining and the lack of flexibility started to make me wonder if I could continue to play there for the long-term.

I was offered an extension to my contract but I hesitated. There were rumours that other teams were interested in me, and I had been talking to players from other clubs and building a picture of the alternative possibilities out there. At the age of 22, I was still somewhat naive and wanted to enjoy life a little more.

Certain aspects of being with Buriram bothered me. They were my employers and they had the right to set the conditions that they felt were necessary for the team to have success on the pitch. However, I couldn't understand why I was only allowed a couple of days to spend time with my family halfway across the world. I couldn't understand why they couldn't let me skip the New Year's party to spend time with my family instead.

This was certainly a factor in my reluctance to commit myself to a new deal and the club wasn't happy with me. I then fell out of favour and was in and out of the team in the first half of the 2014 season. I always felt the main reason was that I hadn't signed a new contract, not because of my form.

While living at the camp had its benefits in the first year, I was ready for more privacy in the second year and, along with teammates Anthony Ampaipitakwong and Top Phataraprasit, we rented a house together. I still had to follow rules around staying in the camp at certain times, but I stayed in the house when I had time off.

After the dominance of 2013, Buriram United were out of sorts at the start of 2014. Osmar moved to FC Seoul and that was obviously a huge loss for the team. There were high hopes that former Arsenal youth striker Jay Simpson would make an impact but things didn't work out for him. There was a lot of pressure to repeat the success of the previous year and we didn't respond positively in the first six months.

During that time, I received a call from Zico who made it clear that he wanted me in the squad for two big tournaments that year—the Asian Games and the AFF Cup. However, he also made it clear that it might not be possible to pick me if I wasn't playing regularly. As a result, I called my agent and asked what my options were. He made it clear that I should either sign the contract extension with Buriram or look for a loan deal. I preferred the latter option.

My relationship with Buriram had become strained to the point that I no longer felt comfortable there. I probably didn't handle the contract situation very well and if I could go back, I would certainly do things differently. I would also tell my agent to handle it differently. Rolf is European so his style of communication may have been culturally insensitive in a country where saving face is so important.

One of the main things I learned in Thailand was the importance of communicating messages in a certain way. Having only been in the country for a year at the time, I lacked the skills to help me deal with a sensitive situation effectively. Of course, we all learn from mistakes and experience, and that was one example.

Another thing I learned was that with my character and with the profile I was developing off the pitch, the intensity and win-at-all-costs attitude of Buriram was maybe not the right environment for me as a person. I needed time for other things than football. Winning has always been really important to me and staying at the club where success looked guaranteed seemed a logical choice. However, the experience also taught me for the first time that winning might not be everything.

I wish I had left the club on better terms, but I had to focus on both my career and personal happiness. I will always be grateful to Buriram United for the opportunities they gave me. They were the reason I came to Thailand and went on to enjoy a great lifestyle in a country that I love. I still have a good relationship with Newin and when we meet, he's always interested in how I'm doing. I'm glad we still have our relationship because leaving the club was difficult. I can't deny that there was a sense of relief when I left, but I do have regrets about how it ended.

Suphanburi agreed to take me on loan and I had a great time there in the second half of the year. I immediately felt at ease because I could feel a lot of trust in the people around me, whereas at Buriram, I always felt intense pressure and high expectations.

I also had a great coach at Suphanburi. Like Davide Morandi at Lugano, Velizar Popov seemed to intuitively know how to get the best out of me. Popov was an emotional guy and there was a lot of screaming and shouting, but he was also very supportive and he played a big role in putting a smile back on my face and helping me end the year so strongly.

At the time, it felt like Suphanburi had aspirations to be one of the biggest clubs in the country. The fans were great, the stadium was decent and the playing surface was excellent. They also had a great purpose-built training facility that showed the club had invested in infrastructure. Like Buriram, Suphanburi is a relatively small town, without the traffic congestion of Bangkok. The people are friendly and give you words of encouragement if they see you on the street.

A big difference was that I had my own house and only had to spend one night in a hotel with the team before games, in contrast with the three-night requirement at Buriram. It was also nice to be closer to Bangkok and to have a bit more time to myself and to spend with friends. I had a more normal life, but I still maintained my focus on football.

I was playing well for Suphanburi and at times I felt that the game was slowing down to allow me to play at my pace. I always seemed to manage to choose the right passes at the right times.

Then came the Asian Games in September 2014. Like the SEA Games, it was an U23 tournament, so it felt a little like we were getting the 2013 SEA Games gang back together.

The preparation camp was really hard work, but it paid off during the tournament as we were so fit and could run all day. We played aggressive, pressing football. I think we surprised a lot of people with our playing style and we really started to connect with the fans.

Zico was really important to this connection. As a legendary figure in Thai football, he already had everyone's respect but he was the perfect fit as the national team's head coach. He formed very good relationships with the players and he knew how to deal with the media and get them on our side.

We helped Zico by doing our bit on the pitch and, after getting through the group stage, we beat China and then Jordan to reach the semi-finals. As well as being young, you could just feel there was great hunger in our squad and a lot of big characters were emerging.

Another key element in our success was the fact that Zico was allowed to do his job without interference. He knew the style of play that suited us and, as long as he was getting results, he was left alone to implement his way of doing things on and off the pitch. Not every coach has that luxury. We played really well in the semi-final against South Korea and we were a little unfortunate to lose.

However, finishing in the top four was such an important part of the process of returning Thailand to the top of Southeast Asian football.

Everyone was pulling in the same direction and it was a rare period of harmony within the national team setup.

The Asian Games was also a great life experience. It has the feel of the Olympic Games as you meet all sorts of athletes from different countries in a communal dining area.

During that time, my off-field profile really took off as well. When I was going down to the dining hall one day, some of my teammates approached me and told me my Instagram account was being flooded with new followers. I looked at it and I had about half a million new followers.

Instagram wasn't something I had been using much, but it was much bigger in Asia than Europe at the time. I think I had about 10,000 followers before the Asian Games and they were mainly connected to football. The surge in my followers during the event was apparently due to the fact that a famous Thai actress, Gubgib, had posted my photo with the caption, 'He stole my heart'.

When I returned from the Asian Games, I signed a three-year contract with Suphanburi. We finished the league in sixth place but it wasn't unreasonable to believe that the club might be challenging teams like Buriram and Muangthong in a couple of years.

It's fair to say that life was good at this point both on and off the pitch. Unfortunately, some dark times were just around the corner.

CHAPTER 5
Injury pain —
A career put on hold

There were so many positive things happening in my life in the second half of 2014, but something wasn't right. My right knee was bothering me and, as much as I wanted to, I couldn't just ignore it and play through the pain.

It's impossible to say exactly how it happened, but I couldn't shake the feeling that it might have dated back to the injury I suffered at Buriram. A doctor suggested I probably had a tear in my cartilage that was just getting bigger and bigger. My injury was no doubt exacerbated by the heavy load of 2014 that included both the Asian Games and the AFF Cup. It felt like I had done three pre-seasons in the space of six months.

The pain really started when I returned from the Asian Games. My knee was swelling up like a balloon and there was a lot of inflammation and fluid. It was clear that the injury had to be addressed, but I wanted to wait for the right moment to do it instead of killing the momentum.

I managed the injury and got through the end of the league campaign with Suphanburi before heading straight to the preparation camp for the AFF Cup. I was lucky that Andy Schillinger was working with the national side at the time because he is great at managing injuries and rehab. Without him, I don't think I would have been able to play in the tournament.

Throughout the event, I had treatment on my knee three times a day—morning, afternoon and evening. I sat out the dead rubber against Myanmar in the group stage, but I took painkillers before each game I played. I felt a lot of pain after every match, especially after the semi-final clash against the Philippines on artificial grass. But somehow, maybe because of adrenaline and the painkillers, the injury didn't really bother me during matches. I did my best to take good care of my knee and I had a lot of support. I figured that once the tournament was over, I would have the necessary time to rest and recover.

After the euphoria of the AFF Cup win, I really felt on top of the world and stopped thinking about my knee. I went back to Switzerland for Christmas, and my intention was to return to Thailand on January 6 for pre-season at Suphanburi. Without intensive training and regular matches, there was no more pain. That was a very encouraging development and it kind of convinced me that the issue had been resolved.

Although it seemed that the rest had done me good, my agent advised me to get an MRI scan on my knee, just to confirm there was no serious damage and, hopefully, to put our minds at ease. Wishful thinking!

On January 5, I went for the scan and the results brought me back down to earth. Normally, when you need an MRI, you already know something is wrong and you expect to be out injured for a couple of months. However, on this occasion, I went looking for confirmation that everything was okay.

The report from my doctor was a huge shock. I was with my ex-girlfriend, waiting for the results of the scan when he came to see us. The look on his face immediately told me that something was seriously wrong and I began to feel very uncomfortable. I asked him to be straight with me and he told me it didn't look good at all.

I asked if that meant I might be out for two to three months and he just responded that he was unable to give me a timeline. That was when reality hit. No timeline could only mean a very long time out. The doctor was obviously used to communicating this kind of bad news and he gave me time to process the information and get over the initial shock before explaining it in greater detail.

He broke the news that there was a hole in my cartilage with a diameter of about 5 cm. When I asked about my options, he told me it depended on how long I wanted my career to last, which really shook me. I was just about to turn 23, so my only thought was to play for as long as physically possible. Being asked to consider how long I wanted to play was such a sobering experience. It was devastating and a little surreal.

As soon as I left the hospital, I got on the phone to inform my family and then my agent. My head was still a little fuzzy at the time. Just hours beforehand, I had been looking forward to another great season and hoping to be one of the faces of Thai football again. With Suphanburi on the rise, there was also a strong possibility of competing for trophies.

At moments like those, you realise that while a career as a professional football player is a privilege and a dream job, it is also a very fragile one. Everything can change very quickly because of one bad tackle, one awkward landing or just when joints or muscles cannot cope with the physical demands of being a professional athlete.

After I had taken time to digest the grim news, the doctor recommended a recently developed technology. At that time, that kind of surgery could only be done in Switzerland, Germany and the USA. I listened carefully to the explanation that the procedure would require the growth of new cartilage for a month. When it was ready, it would be implanted into my knee as what the doctor called a "baby cartilage". It would then grow inside the knee for eight to 12 months before it would be possible to really start putting pressure on the knee again and consider going back to proper training.

So that was it. I was looking at a year out of the game at least. I had been in the form of my life during the previous six months and had been one of the stars of the AFF Cup. The timing couldn't have been worse.

While it was an awful situation to be in, following discussions with my parents and my agent, the decision to have the surgery was an easy one. I was lucky I had just signed a three-year contract with Suphanburi, so I had some job security. It was also such an exciting stage of my career that there was huge motivation to try and get back to where I was as quickly as possible.

An alternative option was to have a less invasive surgery. It would have involved drilling small holes in my knee cartilage to improve blood flow. That would potentially have seen me back playing much sooner, but it would probably have meant another operation would be necessary just two or three years down the line, so it didn't appeal at all. I would maybe have accepted that option at the age of 30 when my career would only have another two or three years. However, at the age of 23, it would have felt like giving up on my dreams and I wasn't ready for that.

But deep down, I was still gutted when I thought about some of the opportunities I was going to miss. Thailand's 2018 World Cup qualifying campaign was about to start and there had been tentative contact with some Japanese clubs. It always seems futile to speculate about what might have been, but I remain convinced that had I not suffered my injury, I would have been one of the first Thai players to play in the J.League.

I was under contract with Suphanburi but after my performances in the AFF Cup, a few clubs contacted my agent to ask about me. It never came to anything but the interest was there and who knows how it might have developed if I had not spent almost 18 months out of the game.

The football world is full of players who talk about the career they might have enjoyed, had it not been for bad luck with injuries. I have never really wanted to dwell on what might have been but, every so often, I can't help thinking about the opportunities that may have come my way. At the time though, I just had to accept it and do my best to get back on the right track.

I returned to Thailand a week later than planned so I could break the news to Suphanburi. It was obviously a huge blow to the club as well. That year, they had hoped to be pushing hard to be among the top teams in the country and the intention had been to build the team around me. In addition to my potential influence on the pitch, I was also a major marketing asset. As a consequence, I was asked not to reveal anything to the media about the injury. The club had received some big sponsorship offers and felt that many of them were down to my presence. There was a need to be pragmatic.

One of the sponsorship deals was with Swiss luxury watchmaker Hublot and it was strongly linked to me and the country of my upbringing. Suphanburi didn't want to risk that or any other deals so it was a little difficult to communicate with the fans and the media as I had to be very careful about what I said. A lot of rumours were swirling around about the seriousness of my injury, so it was a very tough time. It would have been nice to communicate frankly about my situation, but it just wasn't feasible.

After my trip to Thailand, I had to return to Switzerland for an arthroscopy that would fully reveal the extent of my injury. They took some cartilage out and then I had to wait another month for some of my cartilage to grow back before the second operation. During that month, I went back to Thailand and did a commercial for Nivea and helped Suphanburi with some of our promotional activities for the upcoming season. Despite my personal difficulties, I was still well aware of the commitments I had made, so I tried to fulfil as many of them as possible.

I knew I was going to be out for a very long time—at least a year—but I couldn't talk about it in the media or let the fans know. As a club, Suphanburi dealt with the situation very well and that made me more determined to do whatever I could to help them. I knew I still had responsibilities from a marketing point of view because the club had invested a lot in me and suddenly, I was going to be out for over 12 months. It was important to show appreciation and give something back. My injury obviously wasn't my fault, but I still felt somewhat guilty for letting them down just after signing my contract.

It was very frustrating for me to look on, somewhat helplessly, but to this day I am grateful for the support of the club during such a difficult time. Perhaps the biggest challenge contractually was determining who paid for my surgery and rehabilitation. There were some issues between Suphanburi and the Football Association of Thailand as I had suffered the injury on international duty at the Asian Games, so there was a bit of a grey area in terms of who was responsible.

There were so many things swirling around my head but my focus had to be my health. I was still very much in demand in Thailand. I was getting so many offers to do commercials, attend events and engage in other promotional activities, but I had to say no to most of them because it became difficult to focus on my recovery. It was a tough decision, but I chose to do my rehabilitation after surgery in Switzerland because it was important to have my family and friends around me. At the time, it seemed the right decision, but in hindsight, perhaps it created unnecessary problems further down the line.

In my mind, it was important to avoid distractions as I focused on getting fit and, while Suphanburi were supportive, I can see how it might have looked from outside the club. What was wrong with doing the rehab in Thailand to be around the team? What did Switzerland offer that Thailand couldn't? It's too late now to change that decision, but it did come back to haunt me somewhat.

In terms of the payment for surgery, it was finally agreed that Suphanburi would pay the fee. My agent and I managed to find a surgeon who, due to some personal connections, would perform the operation for half the price we were originally quoted in a different hospital, so I was happy to save the club some money.

As the date of the surgery approached, I was in Switzerland waiting while my new cartilage was growing in a fridge. On the day of the operation, I received a call from the hospital at 7am and they told me the fee had not been received. They said that if the money did not come through in the next two hours, the cartilage would have to be thrown away and the process would have to start all over again. It was not a simple procedure and there were very strict guidelines to follow. We couldn't just reschedule for the next day or the next week.

I called Suphanburi but no one answered. When I finally got a response, the person on the other end of the line didn't know what to do or who to ask. In the end, I had to pay the fee out of my own pocket. It was obviously very risky, but my health was the most important consideration. I was already going to spend a long time out of the game and did not want to extend that unnecessarily.

To be fair, I did get my money back from the club. It took almost two years, but we got there in the end...

After the operation, I had to spend three months with crutches. I had a machine on my bed that enabled me to exercise my knee to ensure I didn't lose too much muscle. As a kid, I had thought a broken bone in my foot was a serious injury. However, this was on a different level.

But there were certain similarities with being a kid again. I was back staying with my dad and he had to work hard to take care of me. It was back to the old routine of him driving me around from place to place when I needed a lift. It was funny in some ways and it was good to spend a lot of time together again. I felt a little guilty about putting him through it but, as always, he was very supportive and never complained. We also got to watch plenty of sports on TV together, just like the good old days.

I tried to put a brave face on as much as I could, but some days were a real struggle. The uncertainty around the rehab methods was very difficult. Because it was such a new procedure, everything was somewhat experimental. The doctors didn't really know what was best for me. For nine months, the cartilage was growing and they kept using the analogy of a baby learning to walk—we know the approximate age when a baby takes its first steps, but we don't know the exact age.

During the first two to three months of my rehabilitation, it was difficult to know what to do with my time as I needed my crutches and had limited freedom and independence. While I thought doing the rehab in Switzerland was the best move because I had my family around me, I began to have doubts. Not only was I not playing football, but I was also losing touch with the club and my teammates.

On the commercial side, I also missed out on so many opportunities. I had convinced myself that the best thing was to focus on getting better, to enjoy spending time with family and friends and to avoid distractions. This was nice at the beginning and there was a sense of relief that, for the first time since my early childhood, I didn't have constant pressure to perform well as a player. However, the situation also affected my motivation and it would probably have been better to return to Suphanburi sooner.

At home, I was usually alone. From Monday to Friday, life went on as normal for everyone else. They went to work and had regular things to do, while my only job was to focus on the recovery of my knee. I had regular physio and did my exercises, while also treating my knee appropriately with cold compresses or some heat.

I got really bored, really fast. I watched a lot of TV, became a little anxious at times about my future and had a mental battle to stay positive. Equally, when you are in a club environment and you cannot play, it's very difficult to be around the other members of the squad. It's also tough to go and watch them play at the stadium, whether they are winning or losing. It's just so lonely to be separated from the group and unable to contribute. It's really a no-win situation. You just have to get through it.

It didn't help that pressure began to build on social media as the 'haters' and trolls began to take an interest. There was so much focus on me around that time that my absence was always going to make news. The fact that it wasn't feasible to reveal the extent of my injury or the length of my absence meant that rumours continued to spread. There were some ridiculous suggestions that I just wanted to have a longer holiday at home, or that I wanted to party after the AFF Cup victory.

It was completely understandable that Suphanburi wanted to protect their business interests by keeping my condition quiet, but it certainly didn't help at times.

Once I was mobile again, on my trips back to Thailand I had become such a well-known face that I couldn't eat in peace in a public place or visit shopping malls. I'm not sure if people recall the chaos around my life during that period, but I became one of the most famous faces in the country.

Given my relative youth and the fact I was recovering from such a serious injury, it was sometimes very difficult to keep a smile on my face when dealing with the public when I wasn't really in the mood. On some occasions, I would be in the middle of eating and had a mouthful of food when someone would approach me and take a picture. It wasn't easy to keep my cool every time it happened.

I admit that I got annoyed about it on certain days. Looking back, it was a mistake to let my emotions get the better of me and lash out at people but that was part of the learning process I had to go through. It's always important to remind myself that I am where I am because of the fans.

Back in Thailand, I gradually started to reintegrate myself at the club and do a bit of light training. I made sure I met the club president regularly and did some work with the physios when I was in Suphanburi.

I was still doing some commercial work as well as attending some promotional events. To some fans, that was not a good look. Without full disclosure of the precise nature of my injury, they just didn't understand how I could be doing that kind of thing but not playing. That wasn't exactly logical as rocking up to a product launch and standing or sitting around for a while was a world away from high-intensity training and playing.

Slowly but surely, steps were taken to get me closer to a return. I started running on the Alter G anti-gravity treadmill as one of the first steps in my recovery but it wasn't until the end of 2015 that I started running on grass.

There was still a long way to go, but it never crossed my mind that I wouldn't be able to play professional football again. The only doubt I had was whether I would be able to reach the same level again. Some of that pressure came from inside me, but it was also coming from other angles.

I also missed the natural therapy that comes from playing football. Ever since I was a kid, I had always forgotten any troubles I had during matches. Playing just takes your mind to a different place, so without that escape, it was so much tougher from a mental point of view.

At times, I felt lucky that I couldn't read Thai as the social media noise continued about my absence. I was reliably informed that it was all speculative and mostly inaccurate. I didn't like people lying about me, but I didn't really care about those online rumours as they were coming from keyboard warriors, not people whose opinions mattered. My mum read some of the negative comments, but she's a strong woman and didn't let them bother her.

However, the attitude of some of my teammates did disappoint me. It sometimes felt like jealousy. I understood there was a disproportionate focus on me even when I wasn't playing. Of course, that seemed a little unfair to the players who were giving 100% on the pitch every week. At the same time, the attention was not something I chose. It was something that came to me.

While the social media hate from fans was something I could learn to live with and ignore, I did feel hurt by the way some teammates behaved. I was genuinely sad about it. You see your teammates more often than your family, so their opinions matter. Things were never said to my face, but I was well aware that stuff was said behind my back.

I was trying my best to accelerate my comeback so that I could help the team, but I felt there was unnecessary pressure from some players. I was struggling with my weight as I had put on quite a few pounds during the period when I couldn't move much. It wasn't like I was doing it on purpose, as every person has a different metabolism. Some people can eat whatever they want but always seem to remain slim. That's not me. Since being a kid, I have always had to watch what I eat to ensure I stay in shape. If I couldn't be active for around eight months, my weight was naturally going to increase.

It did help though that during my absence, the team did very well and eventually finished third in the Thai League in 2015. If I had been fit and taken my form from the end of 2014 into the new season, we could even have been challenging for the title. It's another 'what might have been' scenario, but it is something I have thought about.

At the beginning of 2016, there was some light at the end of the tunnel as I joined the team for pre-season training. I knew that the first game of the season in early March would come too soon for me, but it felt like a huge step to be back and at least looking forward to being involved at some stage in the first half of the season.

CHAPTER 6
The comeback

Coming back after 16 months out, football changes. I had left the game on a high, feeling almost superhuman. When I returned, I could barely catch my breath and opponents flew past me.

I could run, but my reading of the game and my anticipation felt different. Things that had been second nature suddenly required a lot of effort.

It took so long for me to readjust to the pace of the game and that was a real shock. I knew that it would be tough, but I had no idea it would be such a struggle. It wasn't just the physical aspect, which was never my strong point anyway, it was also a huge challenge mentally.

The shock to my system immediately made me doubt whether the operation had been the right decision. It crossed my mind that taking the shorter-term view and the less- intrusive operation might have allowed me to play at a higher level for longer. Of course, that might have meant needing to have a more complicated operation two or three years later, but at least I might have enjoyed greater success.

To this day, the dilemma still plays on my mind at times. Did I do the right thing? For my career, it probably wasn't the best move, but for my long-term health, it was surely the right thing to do. That's what I have to believe anyway.

It seemed unfair that many fans seemed to expect me to return to my previous form so soon, but I guess few had any true understanding of what I had been through just to play again.

Perhaps I was lucky to be in the Thai League and not playing at a higher level in Europe or Japan where I may not have returned at a strong enough level and may have had to drop down divisions. It would have been so difficult to return after 16 months out of their leagues. I have friends who suffered serious cartilage injuries and they never came back at the same level.

As my return got closer, the club arranged a friendly against Simork FC, our feeder club. It was April 2016. I had not played an organised match since December 2014, and I have to admit I was a bit anxious, even though it was a meaningless match against lower-league opponents.

I struggled for breath in that match. We had changed head coach at the start of the year and the new man had to get a look at me as well. Sergio Farias had come in and would have been well aware of the attention surrounding my return to action. He would not have been impressed with what he saw that day. I was just happy to be back, but it was surprising to feel just how much a long time out could change your perception of the pace of the game.

Again, it was the mental side that was difficult. I had always thought of myself as having a high football IQ, something that had given me an edge over opponents since I was young. That was why I was part of a team that won the U-17 World Cup and why the top side in Thailand pushed hard to sign me.

However, I realised that while I might be able to get back into the right physical shape more quickly, catching up on the mental side would take significantly longer. It probably took almost a full year to feel like I was back at the top of my game.

When I finally did make my comeback in a competitive match, it was a substitute appearance against Army United in May 2016 and I will never forget the reception I got. The whole stadium cheered and it made me realise why I went through what I had been through. It reminded me that it had been worth every second, despite all the pain and frustration. But there were still a lot of obstacles ahead.

As my comeback progressed in 2016, after games my knee still felt like it hadn't completely healed and there were other aches and pains as my body tried to rebalance itself. You can do as much training and physical conditioning as you want, but the only thing that can really take you to the right level is playing high-intensity games. It felt like I needed at least 15 games in my legs to get me back to full match fitness.

Despite the challenges, there was still a lot of support and the interest from fans was overwhelming at times. After games, I would be the only one left outside the stadium taking pictures with them. I didn't always want to do that as I would still be sweating from my warm-down session, and I might have also been smarting because of a poor result. Smiling for the cameras when you're in a foul mood because you or the team have played badly was not always easy, but it had to be done. It was always important to remember that a smile from me could make a fan's day.

I had to give something back to the fans who had supported me through the dark times. When I was in the right mood, I enjoyed the interaction with fans from all over the country, and it was flattering to receive such interest. But it was still difficult to react in a polite manner in certain places when some fans could be pretty rude. It was never a problem when they apologised for disturbing me and asked if it was okay to take a photo. That's absolutely fine.

However, it wasn't unusual for some people to just grab you and say, "Let's have a photo". I might be in the middle of talking to friends, having a coffee or, as I mentioned before, even sitting with a mouthful of food. In those situations, I would probably just glare at the person and inside I was thinking, *'What the hell is wrong with you? Can you not just show a little respect?'*

At the same time, I had to remember that in some cases, these people were very nervous and not thinking straight. The behaviour is probably not intentionally rude but a result of nerves and poor social skills. It still happens now and sometimes I might be smiling but a little sarcastic and say, "Are you asking me for a photo or are you telling me to pose for a photo?"

However, they don't really get that if I say it in English. They just laugh and take the photo.

A reminder of my own responsibilities came in 2017 when David Beckham was in Bangkok shooting a commercial for an insurance company. I was staying in a hotel and Beckham was in the coffee shop downstairs. Becks was one of my heroes growing up —one of the reasons I became a footballer. I had great admiration for his style of play and also his fashion sense and off-field swagger. When I went to the coffee shop, I saw him and felt very star struck.

I felt very nervous about approaching him, but it was possibly a once-in-a-lifetime opportunity to meet one of my all-time heroes. Despite his celebrity, I had also been led to believe that he was pretty modest and approachable. Eventually, I plucked up the courage to go and ask for a photo. When I started walking towards him, I was intercepted by two minders who told me that Beckham would not be interrupted while eating. I was really disappointed because it would have been very special to have met such an icon.

I am not comparing Beckham's level of global fame to my more localised celebrity, but the principle is the same. If a fan comes up to me and asks for a photo, but I'm in a bad mood and say, "not today", I could cause real disappointment and embarrassment. Since that experience with Beckham, I have been more conscious than ever of the need to give fans a photo whenever they want one, whatever the circumstances. That moment in the coffee shop certainly changed my perspective.

A friend of mine stayed in Bangkok for a couple of years and was used to seeing me approached by strangers and observing my reactions. He returned after an absence of several years and noticed the difference in how I handled these situations. Even when people disturbed me at the wrong moments, I always remained calm and courteous. It was nice to hear that as it was a confirmation of having gone through a learning process and adapting as a result.

Things got especially crazy at away games in places like Sukhothai or

Chiang Rai. Even the opposition fans wanted to meet me and get their photos, such was my celebrity at that time. It felt strange as it seemed to separate me from my teammates as I was the only one getting all that attention. I was very conscious of it and perhaps some jealousy was there but, as I said, it was not my choice to have the attention. To an extent, it caused tension within the squad.

Because of this distance to my teammates, I probably became less open, which may have led them to perceive it as arrogance. It wasn't arrogance but a certain wariness as, without naming names, I knew what some of them had been saying about me when I was out injured.

I had over a million followers on social media and everything I did was scrutinised, which obviously wasn't always welcome, but was what my life had become. If the team lost, I was the one to blame, but when we won, I got the most praise. Either way, it may not have been deserved but critiques of my performances seemed to either be very positive or very negative. There was never a middle ground.

There were no real concessions for the fact that I was still finding my feet after a long absence. Expectations of me seemed to be as high as they had been before my injury, if not higher, and I couldn't always live up to them. The pressure was intense and I sometimes struggled mentally, being very conscious of the differences in how I was playing and what I had been capable of before the injury setback. It was partly my own fault as I put myself under pressure. Even at that time, my mind was focused on taking Suphanburi to a higher level and winning trophies. I should have simply focused on one game at a time and looked for a gradual improvement rather than long-term goals.

On the pitch, things were certainly moving in the right direction and a real turning point came at the end of July. In a match we ultimately lost 3-2 against Super Power Samut Prakan, I scored twice, and after the game I received a call from Zico. He told me he wanted me back in the Thailand squad but, for his own peace of mind, he wanted to run me through some fitness tests.

Out of respect for him, I took the tests privately and passed without any issues. The AFF Cup was coming up at the end of the year and Thailand had reached the final stage of World Cup qualifying for just the second time in their history, meaning some big matches were on the horizon.

It was my good fortune that the national team still had the same coach—someone who trusted and valued me. However, my form was also getting better and I was starting every match, so I earned my place in the squad. My selection wasn't a sentimental move at all, but from a psychological point of view, it gave my confidence a huge lift and maybe that was part of Zico's thinking. I certainly felt a lot of gratitude for the faith he was showing in me and I was determined to pay him back.

My comeback story was also useful for the media as it generated a few headlines and made an interesting subplot to a series of matches that autumn. However, most importantly, I had to perform. While my return was intriguing for fans and media, there was considerable scepticism, so there would certainly be a backlash if I played poorly.

I made the squad for the first double header of the World Cup qualifying group. It was a little strange going back to international duty as there were a lot of new players in the squad and the vibe had changed significantly. There didn't seem to be the same sense of unity, but the quality was definitely higher.

Teerasil and Theerathon, who had missed out on the AFF Cup in 2014, were better than ever, and younger players like Chanathip, Sarach and Adisak had benefited from two additional years of experience and were improving all the time. While the standards had been raised, the various members of the squad were a little more focused on themselves rather than the group. My feeling was that some players were more concerned with how they performed personally rather than the goals of the team.

It was a bit of a shock for me to come back to this change in atmosphere. Perhaps it was naive of me to think it would be just like it was back in 2014. And perhaps the nostalgia for such good times affected my judgement.

But what happened on the pitch was more important and we made an encouraging start to our campaign. Even though we lost to Asian heavyweights Saudi Arabia in Riyadh, we competed well. I came on as a substitute and we only lost after a late and very controversial penalty before being denied a stonewall penalty of our own. It was a really hard loss to take.

A few days later, I started against Japan on a very rainy night in Bangkok. This time, we couldn't really complain about the match ending in a 2–0 defeat to another of the continent's top sides, but it was another personal milestone as I started a game for Thailand for the first time in 21 months. It felt like I had passed a test and that led to my selection for the AFF Cup squad later in the year.

In many ways, the AFF Cup campaign in 2016 was a mental battle for me. I was delighted to be in the squad but, unlike two years earlier, I wasn't a nailed-on starter. I was in and out of the team during the tournament, so it was especially satisfying that Zico showed faith in me in the decisive second leg of the final against Indonesia. It really reinforced the impression that my career was finally back on track, almost two years on from hearing the devastating news of my serious injury.

We had a really strong squad for that tournament. Even if the results of some individual fixtures don't suggest it, our eventual triumph felt inevitable. Before each match, we felt certain we would win. Even when we made hard work of some games, we knew we would prevail in the end. In the final match of the group stage, we put more or less a second-string side out against the Philippines and we still managed to take the three points.

Indonesia managed to beat us 2–1 in the first leg of the final, which surprised everybody, but there was no panic on our side. We knew we were the better side and that we could finish the job when we welcomed them to Bangkok. The defeat perhaps opened the door for me to return to the starting lineup in the second leg and, once again, I was grateful to Zico for trusting me in a big match like that.

However, winning the tournament after beating the Indonesians 2–0 didn't have the same feeling as it did in 2014. Two years previously, we went into the event with hope but not a lot of expectation. This time, anything but victory would have been considered a failure and a crushing disappointment.

Of course, we were satisfied and somewhat relieved but there was not the same outpouring of joy as there had been in Kuala Lumpur in 2014. Thailand was also still mourning the death of King Rama IX, so celebrations were inevitably muted.

While it might have lacked the magic of the previous victory, it remains a highlight of my career given the context. It helped me to answer a lot of questions about my ability to play at that level again and it really set me up for the next season.

Coming off the back of that second AFF Cup triumph, I was flying in pre-season for Suphanburi. In contrast to much of the previous six months, I was in really good shape. In the first half of 2017, I had the most assists for Suphanburi and was one of the top creators in the league.

I made the squad for the next two World Cup qualifiers, but we were again punished for a lack of experience at that level. I came on as a second-half substitute at home to Saudi Arabia and looked on helplessly as our opponents hit us with two late sucker punches to win 3-0. In Japan, I watched from the bench as we battled gamely but were comprehensively outclassed and eventually lost 4-0. For context, the Japanese had Southampton's Maya Yoshida, Inter Milan's Yuto Nagatomo, Borussia Dortmund's Shinji Kagawa and English Premier League champion Shinji Okazaki in their starting XI. The gulf in quality was there for all to see. Nevertheless, the armchair critics were sharpening their claws.

Days later, Zico quit. It hit me hard as he had been such a positive influence for me and many others. It was really unfair that he was being criticised for defeats to two Asian heavyweights.

Back in 2014, throughout that hugely successful year, no one had ever tried to interfere with what Zico was doing and we delivered as a team on the pitch. Since my return to the national team, there seemed to be more people around trying to influence things. Zico remained respectful but it didn't seem to help that other people might have been in his ear.

One example came before one of the World Cup qualifying matches.

Zico had a close relationship with Leicester City and one of the staff from the English champions did an analysis of our opponents before we played them. Zico presented it to us as part of our preparations.

Literally a few hours later, a senior member of the Thailand setup presented his own analysis, and it was the complete opposite of what Zico had told us. I knew then that the interference had gone too far. Things had been working so well and certain people just seemed to want to claim their share of the glory, which was completely counterproductive.

It was sad to see such disrespect towards Zico after everything he had achieved for the national team, not just as a coach, but also during a great playing career. The football he encouraged also brought a lot of interest back from the fans. We were obviously not the strongest team in defence, but his style was not to sit deep and hope to steal a goal and win 1–0. It was expansive, attacking football. We suffered some heavy defeats but he did not compromise and we also had some great moments.

During my spell on the sidelines, the atmosphere at the Rajamangala Stadium was absolutely electric when we came back from 2–0 down to draw 2–2 with Iraq. I was on the bench when we went toe-to-toe with Australia and were unfortunate not to take all three points, having to settle for another 2–2 draw. They were great occasions for the supporters and much of that was down to the fearless way we played under Zico.

You could understand some of the criticism aimed at the coach. It was clear that, while we were capable of playing some nice attacking football at times, we were often far too open at the back and stronger teams ruthlessly exposed us. However, as is often the case in football, his departure was not handled well and left a bad taste.

With the benefit of hindsight, it can't really be claimed that pushing Zico out was the right thing to do. When he left, a lot of the hype around the national side went with him.

Milovan Rajevac came in and, understandably, put the focus on tightening up the defence. It was pragmatic football, but such a contrast to "Zico-ball". Like most new coaches, Rajevac wanted to do things his way and, unfortunately, I was not part of his plans even when I was in great form later on for Muangthong United.

There may have been a perception that I was one of Zico's favourites, along with Kroekrit Thaweekarn and Mongkol Tossakrai, but he really got the best out of us. However, we were not going to be Rajevac's favourites. Zico's departure meant my international career was effectively over at the age of 25.

In action for Switzerland against host nation Nigeria in the final of the U-17 World Cup in 2009

U-17 World Champions! Switzerland defeated Nigeria 1-0, 2009 in Abuja

About to take a penalty in the first leg of the Final of the 2014 ASEAN Football Federation (AFF) Cup against Malaysia, 2014

AFF Cup champions after Thailand won 4-3 on aggregate in the two-leg Final, 2014

Pondering what to do from a set piece for Buriram United in 2014

Winners of the Thailand League Cup with Buriram United, 2013

Greeting Japan's superstar Keisuke Honda at a World Cup qualifier in Bangkok, 2016

Celebrating the 2016 AFF Cup win with teammates Tristan Do and Siroch Chatthong

Being greeted pre-match by fans of Muangthong United

Attempting to calm down Muangthong United head coach Mario Gjurovski after Port FC beat their bitter rivals in 2020

In action for Suphanburi FC, 2017

World Cup qualifying match for Thailand vs Japan, 2016

Playing for Thailand vs Malaysia at the AFF Cup, 2014

With teammates Theerathon Bunmathan and Chanathip Songkrasin at Suvarnabhumi Airport in Bangkok

Playing for Port FC vs Chiangmai United, 2021

Staying positive with Port FC, 2021

CHAPTER 7
The move to Muangthong

A glance at my CV tells you that I am not one for staying in the same place for too long. From the days when I became impatient waiting for my big chance at Grasshopper, I have always found myself looking elsewhere to see what might be more motivating or challenging. Most of all, I look for opportunities to improve and battle for trophies.

After the misery of my time out injured and the battle to regain my match fitness, my stock was high again halfway through 2017. I was in good form, and I was one of the Thai League's leading assist providers. Suphanburi had a decent team but I was at a stage of my life when I was restless again and keen to take on a new challenge. And to be very honest, I also wanted to live in Bangkok and avoid having to travel so much.

I was in the final year of my contract, so I knew there could be opportunities to move on. Two teams from the Bangkok area expressed an interest in signing me—Bangkok United and Muangthong United. At the end of the first leg of the 2017 season, I had a slight injury and missed the last few matches. During this spell I entered negotiations with the two clubs and, in the end, I was left to choose between them. They made similar offers and had similar ambitions to be challenging for trophies every year. Both clubs also indicated I would have a key role to play in their ambitious plans.

The offers were attractive in different ways. Many half-Thai friends were at Bangkok United, like Mika Chunuonsee, Antony Ampaipitakwong and Ernesto Phumipha. Teerathep "Leesaw" Winothai was another player

I knew well who was playing there. Those guys would have helped me settle quickly.

Another significant attraction about the 'Bangkok Angels' was the opportunity to play under Mano Polking, the Brazilian head coach at the time. I liked the way his teams played and his players always spoke highly of him. He was a fluent German speaker, so we spoke that language when we had a chance.

On the Muangthong side, they were the reigning Thai champions and the second most successful side in the short history of the league in its current form. The 'Kirins' had been the champions four times in less than a decade while finishing as runners-up on three other occasions. They had a lot of quality players from the national team and some of the strongest foreign players in the league. They were also a more conventional club with their own purpose-built football stadium and a good fan base. Bangkok United's future was possibly a bit more uncertain as they played in the stadium of Thammasat University campus, around 40 km from the centre of Bangkok.

It was such a tough decision to make and, in the end, it came down to small details. When we had some meetings, Bangkok United's representatives asked me to travel to their offices. For the meetings with Muangthong, their people came to us. Although this doesn't seem like a big issue, it just seemed to suggest that Muangthong maybe wanted me that little bit more.

I also had to remind myself that, while playing with Mano Polking was one of my main reasons for considering the Bangkok United offer, in Thai football, a head coach can leave at any moment. I could have moved there and seen Mano sacked a few months later. That didn't happen in the end but I had to take this factor out of the equation.

Muangthong were also better placed in the league at the time. They were in second place behind Buriram and still in both domestic cups so there was still much to play for in that season.

Suphanburi were eventually willing to let me go for a fee and two players, initially for a six-month loan with a view to a permanent deal. While I had spent a lot of my time at Suphanburi injured, it had still been a three-year stay and I really wanted to move on and live a more interesting life in Thailand's capital city. I was in a relationship at the time and the distance between Bangkok and Suphanburi put a strain on that as I was constantly travelling back and forward.

I also wanted to have a better chance of competing for trophies. It felt that at Suphanburi, the president could not give as much of his time to the club as in the past, and the ambitions of the club seemed uncertain. We were drifting away from being a Top Five side to a mid-table team.

I was very grateful to the club for the support they had given when I was going through such a tough time, especially the president. Khun Top is probably the nicest club president I have played under. Maybe I didn't appreciate that enough at the time, but when your mind's made up on a move, it is hard to change it.

The club could feel that I wasn't happy anymore and I was glad that they received a transfer fee for me rather than leaving them for free at the end of my contract. It would have been nicer to leave under better conditions. It had been a club on the rise when I joined, but its gradual decline had begun before I left.

Suphanburi had so much going for them around 2014 and 2015. The town is in a good location, about a 90-minute drive from Bangkok. They had some great facilities, a strong fan base, an excellent club president and a good team manager. However, as is often the case, there were two or three influential individuals at the club who made some questionable decisions. Their influence started to impact the performance of the team and it was clear to see that it wasn't positive.

As club captain, I started to have players come to me to talk about some issues they were having with the club. It became a little draining to have to get involved and it affected the atmosphere and energy around the club. Suphanburi was a great place for me for a while, but things did turn a little sour.

I played with some excellent players, like Sergio Van Dijk, Dellatorre,

Jakkapan Pornsai, Bjorn Lindemann and Jung Myung-oh. It's just a shame that we couldn't build on what we had.

I left despite having a strong position at the club. As captain, I could expect to be one of the first names on the team sheet but that would not necessarily be the case at Muangthong. I knew that with so many big names, I would have to fight for my place, but I had so much self-belief I wasn't concerned.

The first six months at Muangthong were great. We won a lot of games, though it wasn't enough to catch Buriram in the league. One of the highlights was going to Buriram in the League Cup quarter-final and beating them 2–0. We had a great team. Our midfield three in that match was me, Theerathon and Sarach. Teerasil was up front, with Heberty Fernandes and Leandro Assumpcao playing in wide attacking roles. At wing-back, we had Tristan Do on the right and Peerapat Notchaiya on the left. South Korean international Lee Ho was playing the defensive midfield role, while we had a strong centre-back pairing in Naoki Aoyama and Celio Santos, with Kawin in goal. There was quality all over the pitch.

Of course, the League Cup quarter-final win meant that the stakes were higher. In every training session, you had to stand out. In every match, you had to perform because competition was fierce. But I relished the challenge and that first six months went really fast.

It was great to lift another trophy when we won the League Cup final against Chiangrai United, taking revenge for them beating us on penalties in the FA Cup semi-final. That was something I had missed—playing for a team that was a serious contender for honours.

It had been fun but it hadn't been easy. I played regularly but I did not start every game. I was coming into a side that had won the league the previous year and had enjoyed a good ACL campaign at the start of 2017. It would have been naive to think I would just walk into the side but, overall, I think I played well when I had my opportunities. I established myself as a number six in the team, taking responsibility for dictating the tempo as much as I could. I enjoyed playing for a team that usually had the bulk of the possession in a game.

Having agonised over whether to opt for Muangthong or Bangkok United, I felt like I had made the right decision. We had come second in the league, qualifying for the ACL qualifiers, and I had another winner's medal in my pocket. Bangkok United ended the season six points behind us and trophyless.

In addition to the success on the field, in a team that was full of stars, it felt like duties were a bit more evenly shared when it came to interacting with fans and doing promotional activities. The fans wanted photos with all the players—there was no special focus on me. There was less pressure on me during games as well. There was more of a collective responsibility. At Suphanburi, it always felt like people were looking at me to make things happen.

Having commercial interests off the pitch wasn't such an issue either. More of the players at Muangthong were business-minded and had their own things going on social media and earning money from advertising deals. Tristan Do did a car commercial for Ford, while I did one for Suzuki. Theerathon and Sarach also had some deals on the side.

There was also great chemistry among the team. I had a good friendship with Tristan and quickly connected with the Brazilian players. We played lots of video games, like FIFA or Uno, in our downtime. It was great fun.

It didn't seem possible at the end of 2017, but things would quickly start to go downhill. Chanathip's outstanding performances in the 2016 season and the 2017 ACL campaign earned him a loan move to J.League side Consadole Sapporo just before I joined Muangthong. It was tough to lose a player of his quality, but a club should always be able to cope with the loss of one star player. Unfortunately, Chanathip was just the first domino to fall. We soon learned that we would have to start the 2018 league campaign without Theerathon, Teerasil and Kawin as well. They were not just the best Thai players of their generation; they were among the country's best players of all time. We knew it was going to be hard to replace them.

Theerathon and Teerasil headed to Japan to join Chanathip. Theerathon signed a deal with Vissel Kobe—a team that included the World Cup winning talents of Andres Iniesta and Lukas Podolski. Teerasil headed for Sanfrecce Hiroshima, a club that had secured three J.League titles in the previous seven years. Kawin took a different path, moving west to join OH Leuven in Belgium. Seeing great players moving on is part of football and you had to wish them all the best as these were all positive career moves.

However, they left Muangthong with a huge hole in our talent pool and, for me, the situation could have been handled much better. Rather than planning for the season without those players, we held onto Theerathon and Teerasil for the ACL qualifiers. While we dismissed Malaysia's JDT (Johor Darul Ta'zim) in the first qualifier, we had to travel to Japan for a playoff against Kashiwa Reysol. The tournament's playoffs are very much rigged in favour of the stronger countries as they are the hosts of a one-off match.

Our chances of victory were slim and, not surprisingly, we lost. One week later, we had to begin our league campaign without three of our best players. But the expectations on us remained high. There was still pressure on us to win every game, as there is for any big club, but we were not prepared to simply move on without our star players. That was one of the main reasons why our 2018 season unravelled so quickly. The club's social media team seemed to be focused more on posting news of the players who had left, rather than those that had remained on the team.

It was good for Muangthong's profile that they had managed to sell or loan out such high-quality players but once they were out of the door, it was time to focus on the players still at the club. It was almost like we could not make a clean separation and that affected our pre-season preparation. We should have really focused on who was going to step up and take their places, but we just didn't address the issue.

While there were issues with the way the team was prepared for the upcoming season, I had problems of my own. At the first pre-season training session, I had to drop out for the first time in my career. I had spent a month back in Switzerland and when I returned, I was suffering from stomach pain and upper-back pain. It was so severe that I found it difficult to sleep at night. When I ate, the food would not go down.

It was gutting because I had been determined to come into the new season flying. During my holiday, I trained a lot to keep up my fitness but soon I was suffering from health issues that drained my energy. After failing to complete the first two or three training sessions, it was clear that I had a problem.

I went to hospital and they diagnosed it as inflammation and wanted me to take medicine to solve the problem. But things got worse and they decided to do a laparoscopy to see what was wrong with my stomach. The doctor found that I had a bacterial virus. He also told me that my oesophagus had become swollen and had some bleeding.

I was given some antibiotics and couldn't train for a couple of weeks. My whole system had been disrupted but the biggest impact was on my energy levels. I didn't fully recover for a couple of months. It was a really bad start to the year.

I made it onto the bench for the ACL playoff against JDT and then started the match in Japan a few days later, but that wasn't one of my more memorable performances on the back of just a week's preparation.

It set the tone for a difficult season, not just for me personally, but also for the club. I played in most games but we didn't really have a great season as a team and it didn't help that we went through several coaches.

Totchtawan Sripan led us into the new campaign and he had a lot of credit in the bank. He had led the club to the 2016 Thai League title, the last 16 of the ACL in 2017 and the 2016 and 2017 League Cups. But just five matches into the 2018 Thai League season, he was gone after one of the most embarrassing results in the club's short history.

Prachuap FC had just been promoted to the top tier, while we had been runners-up the previous season, and were also the holders of the League Cup. We travelled south to face them at their home stadium and they destroyed us 6–1. It was such a long journey back and I don't remember much about the match. We just fell apart on the night. It was a bit of a nightmare for me personally as I was taken off at half-time when we were already 4–0 down.

Totchtawan offered to quit immediately after the game and he was allowed to go. I wasn't surprised that he decided to jump before he was pushed. He's the type of guy who would want to leave on his own terms, rather than having someone making the decision for him.

That 6–1 result, and Totchtawan's subsequent resignation, was the trigger for the atmosphere around the club to change.

Former Serbia head coach Radovan Curcic took over. I could see that he had played and coached at a high level and, despite some issues with language, I thought I had a really good relationship with him. He was very expressive on the bench and did his best, but you could sense that there were things going on in the background. SCG, our main sponsor, got really involved in everything. They had been dictating where we went for pre-season camp and what kinds of machines we should use in the gym.

For the first time in my career in Thailand, it was unclear who my boss actually was. There seemed to be a lot of different people involved. With Buriram, Newin is always in the background but everyone knows he's in charge. It is clear that he makes the big decisions at the club. At Muangthong, it was much less clear cut. You had the sponsors, various team managers, the president… There was too much going on and then there was the pressure on the team for not performing.

With several of our biggest stars gone, I could feel the spotlight directed more specifically on me and Sarach. We were now expected to make the team tick. But there were some malicious people who suggested that we had a strained relationship off the pitch, and that as a result, we struggled to play together effectively. That was never the case as we have always had great mutual respect, but the rumour was out there and many believed there was some truth in it.

It was one of those years when things never really felt settled and we struggled to find consistency on the pitch. There were positive moments, like the time I scored a double to beat Chainat 2–0 and a 3–2 victory at Port FC in a thrilling match. But there were also more crushing lows, such as 4–0 and 3–0 defeats to Buriram.

At the end of the year, we finished fourth in the league and had gone out of both cups in the last 16. For a club of Muangthong's standards, those results felt distinctly mediocre. We were a staggering 28 points off the top spot, having been champions just two years previously.

Out went Curcic as coach and in came Pairoj Borwonwatanadilok. It was a surprising appointment for most as he had a respectable but generally modest record in Thai football. It didn't suggest we had the ambition to get back to challenging for the title again. He brought Sarawut Treephan with him, and there will be more on him later as our paths would also cross again. It's fair to say that we did not see eye to eye.

I'm not sure if what was happening at the club was part of the reason for me starting to struggle with my motivation. However, for the first time in my career, I could feel my enthusiasm wane. I kept up with training during the off-season but I can't claim I was really looking forward to going back. There was a feeling of negativity around the club and I took my first ever trip to the USA to get away from it all. I enjoyed my time off and when I came back, the new coaching team was in charge.

For the first time in my career, I was made to feel that I wasn't an important part of the club's plans. I really struggled with that and it was a really tough time mentally. I became more impatient and hot-headed and I didn't start many matches in the first half of the season. Since about the age of five, I had been a valued member of every club I played with and also of national teams at various age groups.

The only things that had disrupted my career and prevented me from being a first-choice player had been injuries, but they had only been temporary. Now, despite being fully fit, it was made clear that I was a squad player rather than a member of the first XI, and it hurt. I was on the bench, and I was not happy.

I have huge respect for players who are not playing a lot but can still offer passionate support to the team. That was so difficult for me. Of course, it's part of being a team player, but I found it very difficult sitting on the sidelines and having to be physically and mentally prepared for the possibility that I might be needed at some point in a match.

Pairoj jumped ship just five games into the season, and after a period under a caretaker coach, South Korean Yoon Jong-hwan arrived, but he didn't seem to have me in his plans either.

Coaches always have their preferred players and that's something you get used to. I had been on the other side of it with Zico and coach Tak at Buriram, who both clearly recognised the best in me. I need a coach who trusts me and talks to me. It's important to feel a connection to have the mutual trust that's required in a team.

For the first time in my career in Thailand, I felt disconnected from the coaching team. It felt like other players were being preferred to me, but I was still very much expected to be at the club's service for promotional events and to satisfy sponsors. The club still needed me, but not on the pitch.

It was a real mental struggle to be in that position and it was made worse by the conversations I had with my dad. I tried to explain the situation to him, but there were no clear answers. If Muangthong had been winning games and racking up the points, it would have been a lot easier to accept. I would have recognised that I had to wait for my opportunity to get into a winning team. But they were in free fall towards the relegation zone and I still wasn't being given a chance. I didn't know what I had done wrong.

Yoon Jong-hwan was a completely different personality from Pairoj but his coaching wasn't the best fit for me either. He had a great career as a player and was a technically gifted midfielder. Because of his qualities as a player, I had high hopes that we would connect as there were surely some things we had in common. Surprisingly, as a coach, he was all about running and fitness rather than technique and tactics.

Admittedly, I was at a stage of my career when I had perhaps become a little too self-important and arrogant. I got frustrated too quickly when things weren't going my way. And I have trouble hiding my emotions, which is not always the best characteristic in Thai culture. But it seemed like really bad luck to have a second successive coach who lacked belief in me. However, not everyone sees football the same way, and it was up to me to adapt to the situation. There wasn't much choice.

One positive thing to come out of Yoon Jong-hwan's short stay at the club was the fact that his training got me really fit and that may have helped a lot when the next coaching change saw me get back on track. A stark example of how he trained the team came during the training camp between the first and second half of the season. I am not sure if he knew his time at the club was coming to an end, but he really went for it.

We were at our training camps in the Khao Yai National Park and he worked us ridiculously hard. We had a friendly match at one point and I could hardly feel my legs. None of the players could move freely so our passing was all over the place. We couldn't make simple passes because we were so stiff. It felt like a muscle could pop at any time.

However, with the team in 14th place out of 16 teams after 15 games, it was time for yet another head coach to move on and another one to arrive. But this new appointment showed much more ambition than the previous two. Alexandre Gama had won two Thai League titles and a domestic treble at Buriram, while also lifting two FA Cups and a League Cup at Chiangrai United. The Brazilian had also been in charge of Buriram when they performed extremely well in the group stage of the 2015 ACL, totalling 10 points in a group that included teams from Japan, South Korea and China.

Gama's arrival was an exciting development. I knew him a little from his time at Buriram as I was still there when he joined them in 2014. Because I knew him and was familiar with his style, I quickly went to him to explain that I was ready to learn from him and to do whatever I could for the team. I think he appreciated that and I did my best in training to win his trust. His presence soon helped me to rediscover my love for the game again.

Gama set about refreshing the squad and brought in my friend Ernesto Phumipha. Two Brazilians—Derley and Bruno Gallo—came from Portugal and they added quality and experience to the front line and midfield respectively. On the training pitch and in competition, Gama quickly showed why he had been so successful in Thai football with Buriram and Chiangrai United. Training was more fun again and the team dynamic was much better. I was back in the starting XI.

When he came to the club, we were at the halfway point of the season and in the relegation zone. After we lost at Chonburi in Gama's first match in charge, we won 22 of the next 24 points. A particularly memorable match was the 3–2 victory at home to a title-chasing Bangkok United. We came back from 2–1 down and scored the winner in the last minute on an emotional evening.

It really felt like the magic had returned to the club and, as no team was running away with the league that year, it even seemed vaguely plausible at one stage that we might have a highly unlikely shot at the title.

For me, it seemed that for the first time since Totchtawan had left 18 months previously, the head coach was in charge again. Gama held some of the best training sessions I have ever had, and his teams always play to win. He is not too concerned about how his team achieves its aims or how many goals they score. He just wants the victory and his trophy record speaks for itself.

The Brazilian had a huge impact in a short time and really helped the players rediscover their confidence. He understood how to play to the strengths of the players.

But just as things were going really well again, the good times didn't last. We stumbled in a couple of games to extinguish any hopes of a title, but 10 wins and just one defeat in a 13-game run was beyond anyone's expectations at the 15-game mark. However, I then found myself out of favour again.

I was in the final year of my contract and, after playing for about five or six games under Gama, I asked my agent to enter negotiations with Muangthong about extending my stay. My agent came over, we had talks and we agreed on a long-term deal with a slight salary increase.

We waited for the contract to come through but the weeks went by and nothing happened. We heard on the news that half of our training complex was being sold, suggesting something was going on at the club. My agent called to ask what was happening with the contract and they explained that due to financial issues, they could only offer me a one-year extension rather than a long-term deal. It was unacceptable to me for the club to change its position. I have never allowed myself to be treated in a way that I feel is unfair.

Around the same time, I was also dealt a blow when the squad for that autumn's World Cup qualifiers was announced. Akira Nishino was now in charge of Thailand so it felt like a clean slate and I was playing well in an in-form Muangthong side. I was confident that I would make the squad but Nishino was apparently not convinced. Strangely however, Sarach was selected despite the fact that he wasn't getting a start at Muangthong. It didn't make much sense at the time.

It got a little worse for me because Sarach played really well in the Thailand matches and combined with my contract situation, I knew that would probably see me lose my place for Muangthong as well. And that's exactly what happened.

I was a bit disappointed in Gama because he didn't explain anything to me about the decision to drop me before a match against Buriram. We won the game, so I couldn't really complain about what he had done, but he could at least have offered an explanation. I'm not sure if it had anything to do with the fact that I was stalling on the new contract but it was the beginning of the end.

As I would not sign the contract extension, I was left out for the last few matches of the season, so my journey with Muangthong was over.

CHAPTER 8

The Port years

At the end of 2019, for the first time in my career, I was without a club. It might sound liberating to find yourself free of attachments, but there is also a lot of anxiety. My agent had to really prove his worth by finding me the right deal as I was getting closer to the age of 30. All of my previous career moves had been fairly smooth, so this one was a new experience for both of us.

We were on the phone to each other non-stop. I knew that my form had been patchy over the previous couple of years, which didn't really help my case. We had to find a club that was both attractive to play for and could offer the right package as I have always commanded a higher-than-average salary.

It's important to remember that my salary was not just about my CV as a player and what I could add to the team. I also had significant commercial value as I helped to bring sponsors and fans, and to sell shirts. I didn't want to compromise too much on the salary but we also had to work out what the market was like at that time.

A few offers came in, including one from BG Pathum United and one from Ratchaburi. In the end I chose Port FC, mainly because it was a longer contract. I was actually offered a little more to go elsewhere but the security of a longer-term deal was more important as I approached my 28th birthday. The opportunity to stay in Bangkok was another significant factor.

Port was also a club on the rise at the time. Although there had been instability in the coaching team, a lot had been invested in the playing squad and consecutive third-place finishes demonstrated that they were a team with the potential to challenge for silverware.

However, looking back, I wasn't really thinking straight at the time and I soon realised that it wasn't the smartest career move. I had been keen to stay at Muangthong, especially with Gama still there and having had such a positive second half of the 2019 season. Perhaps I had been too proud when rejecting their offer because of my personal principles and feelings about how I should be treated.

But I burned my bridges and left myself with limited options. There was interest from Indonesia and Malaysia that could have made me more money, but I wanted to stay in Bangkok for personal reasons and also because it allowed me more opportunities to work on lucrative side projects.

It was clear that I wasn't thinking hard enough about the footballing side. Perhaps I was selling my soul by thinking too much about the financial elements instead of just choosing an opportunity to join a club where I would be able to play every week.

The start to my time at Port didn't help. I was late to the pre-season and that perhaps pushed me down the pecking order. But I also hadn't done my homework on the Port squad and that was negligent on my part. I was thinking that with my quality, I could make an impact but I hadn't looked too much at their playing style and the formation they liked to use.

Most Thai clubs use their foreign contingent as the creators and the centre-backs. Wingers and strikers are often from overseas, while the central midfield is more often Thai. This was the case at my previous clubs in the Thai League, but not at Port. Their creative players were Thai wingers, while Sergio Suarez and Go Seul-ki were regular starters in the centre of the park. The other central midfielder was Siwakorn Jakkuprasat, the club captain. It was pretty clear they had not signed me to replace anyone. I was maybe padding out the squad to add some experience and quality, but I was not coming in as a key player. It was my fault I hadn't figured out that I was joining a club with a very settled team. Port was just the wrong fit for me and I should have known that.

Because I started training later than the other members of the squad, I wasn't selected for the first couple of league games in 2020, but I made my debut as a substitute in a 2–1 win at Sukhothai, and I made another substitute appearance in the 1–1 draw at Buriram the following week.

It had been a positive start to the season for the club, having taken 10 out of 12 points, including a draw from what looked like the most difficult fixture on the calendar. In any circumstances, those results would have made the task of breaking into the starting XI difficult. But then came the latest setback—COVID-19.

Just four matches into the 2020 season and my time at a new club, the league was suspended indefinitely. One month later, I was among the first high profile Thais to test positive for COVID.

This was the time of peak COVID hysteria. The news suggested it was potentially very dangerous and things quickly shut down. Much of the population was scared to leave home and did so only to shop for groceries and household necessities. Everyone, it seemed, was terrified of being one of the few to be struck down with the virus. One of them was me.

It was a really weird situation because I had no symptoms. The only reason for taking a test was to be safe and responsible because, with football on hold, I was going to take a short holiday in Koh Samui. It was a shock to be told that I had tested positive.

Once the positive result was confirmed, I was scared to share the news with too many people because at the time, there was a stigma attached to having the virus. Much of that was due to social media hysteria. For some reason, in Thailand it seemed that having COVID was an indication of irresponsible behaviour rather than bad luck, and it generated criticism rather than sympathy.

Despite that context, Port forced me to go public with a message on social media and I was required to make an apology. It was strange for me to apologise as I had done nothing wrong and the message was private information about my health. What difference did my post make to anyone? I was angry about being forced to do it. In the end, symptoms never developed but it was necessary for me to quarantine in a hotel room for two weeks.

During the first COVID wave, like most people, I spent most of my time at home. We had a training plan that our fitness coach sent to us. We did our best to follow that and we also had to make videos with a time lapse to confirm that we had done the training. You just can't compare real training on the field to what we were doing.

It wasn't easy to maintain motivation in those conditions, especially as it was necessary to take a pay cut for the year as well. Of course, that was tough on everyone but it was an unprecedented situation so it was difficult to be too critical. After having COVID, I was more relaxed about it but there was still a lot of fear around me.

When we restarted the season, it was obviously difficult for everyone to rediscover their fitness levels. Having started the season so promisingly, we didn't do so well when we returned to action. Nonetheless, it was a bit of a knee-jerk reaction to get rid of our head coach Jadet Meelarp when we lost at home to BG Pathum United.

It was particularly bad news for me because his replacement was Mr. Sarawut Treephan. He had been assistant to Pairoj for a short time at Muangthong and we never really connected. It's hard to specify what the problems were between us, but it's safe to say that while he was in charge, I was unlikely to become a first-choice player.

I was faced with another difficult period when it felt that no matter how I trained, the same first XI was selected every week. The only changes tended to be linked to injuries or suspensions and there wasn't much rotation of the squad. That approach meant a lot of my time was spent on the bench. Even on one occasion when I got a rare start, I played well but was hooked early in the second half. I was incensed by that as it just felt personal and I was never given any explanations. I called Sarawut later that evening but he had nothing to say to me about his decision to take me off and just pointed out that I earned more money than him. What can you say to that?

Then there was the time I worked really hard to prepare for the ACL campaign at the beginning of 2021. It was exciting to be back in the tournament and, while COVID restrictions made it less competitive and removed the fans from the stadiums, it was still the biggest stage in Asian club football and I wanted to be part of it.

The league season finished at the end of March. We had been pushing for the title at the halfway point but a disastrous run of five defeats in seven matches ended our hopes. Eventually, we finished in third spot but had the consolation of the ACL to look forward to in June.

There were eight weeks to prepare and I really wanted to prove that I deserved a place in the side. I changed my diet and trained so hard to get myself in the best possible shape. I played really well in some pre-season matches and started in all of them. However, they coincided with some national team matches. As soon as the national team players returned from Thailand duty, I was out in the cold again, and not a word was said about it. Sarawut didn't offer any kind of explanation. Again, it felt personal.

We had six ACL matches and I started five of them on the bench. I stayed on the bench for the first three, but I got on a couple of times after that and then played the full match as we smashed Guangzhou's U22 side 5–1. I even scored a goal in that one.

But we went out at the group stage and it felt like a failure. Guangzhou had more or less gifted every other team six points by bringing their youngsters. Cerezo Osaka had been clear favourites to win the group and did so. That meant it came down to the head-to-head matches between us and Hong Kong's ageing Kitchee, and we could only take one point against a side that we should have beaten twice.

When Port offered an extension to my contract at the end of 2021, I was surprised because I hadn't been playing much. Deep down, I knew that taking their offer wasn't a good idea from a footballing point of view as there were no indications that I was going to become a regular part of the team. However, because I knew how the market was going and the fact that COVID was still an issue, I felt like I had to sign the contract. Everyone had been talking about how clubs were struggling for money and that salaries would suffer because they had been receiving less income. As I wasn't playing that much, my market value was certainly not as high as it had been, so I was just grateful to receive an offer.

But I did ask them straight why they wanted to keep me when I didn't seem to be in the head coach's plans. Samut Prakan City were interested and so were Ratchaburi, but I really didn't have to think twice. It made sense to sign when all things were considered even though it looked likely that I wasn't going to become a regular part of the first XI.

I told myself to be philosophical and just enjoy the moments I spent on the field instead of getting frustrated. Everyone had a fresh perspective after COVID. It highlighted just how precarious our profession could be. I had to remind myself that even if things were not going well for me at the club, I was still very lucky to be doing the best job in the world and I had a very nice lifestyle away from football.

I tried my best to stay focused, which wasn't always easy in the circumstances. But there is always hope. I felt really good at the time and was training well. I had been in really good shape since the ACL matches. One thing I have never lacked is self-belief. Even at testing times such as those, I felt that just a couple of good performances might turn things around. I just needed a chance to show what I could do. And I got my chance just days after signing the new deal. We were up against Buriram United at home and I was given what was becoming an increasingly rare start. My opportunity may have come because of an injury or suspension to another player, but I was keen to make the most of it.

In the end, we played pretty well as a team and I was happy with my performance, but Buriram did what they so often do. After a first half where we had just shaded them, they hit us with a couple of sucker punches early in the second half. I was soon substituted as we chased the game and lost 2–0. Things soon went back to normal, with me usually starting games on the bench.

One of the difficult things for me is that I am not the kind of player who is going to come off the bench and make an impact in the last 15 to 20 minutes of a game. Instead, I tended to be used to help us absorb pressure and defend a lead. As a result, if we needed a goal, I tended to be left on the bench.

In a situation like that, it is very hard to make your case to be a starter because you're never going to catch the eye with the difference you make when you come on as a substitute. To develop match sharpness, you need a run of games, not the chance to play the final 10 or 15 minutes of every second or third match. I thought I had earned the chance to start at least two or three games in a row to build match fitness and confidence, but that never seemed to be the opinion of the coach.

It was possibly also the opinion of some of my teammates. Since my arrival at the club, I had never been given the chance to show what I could do. I was always in and out of the team and couldn't live off my former glories. It was such a settled midfield, so there was huge trust in the players who had been occupying the same positions for a couple of seasons or more.

Despite my pledges to be more philosophical, the situation did get me down at times. When you're putting so much in to keep yourself in the best shape every day, but it doesn't seem to help in any way, you start to ask yourself if there's any point.

While I tried to keep things in perspective, it was hard to see the impact it had on the people around me. My parents and my fiancé were upset and frustrated that I wasn't playing and there's no question about it, it was very hard to stay positive.

It's kind of sad because it could have been so much better at Port. They have such an atmospheric little stadium with really passionate fans and it would have been great to become a hero for them. Maybe it wasn't easy for them to accept me in the beginning because I had just played for their bitter rivals, Muangthong. There was also a big delay in seeing me play much because of the COVID break.

I still felt appreciation from many, but the hardcore Port fans may never have become my biggest supporters. That's understandable as I didn't get much game time. I never felt I had the chance to prove myself to them and potentially become one of their favourites.

But they are really great fans and they are what makes Port FC a special club. I would like to have made a better connection with them but when you're sitting on the bench game after game, you're not always in the mood to join the squad for a lap of honour. At times when I was particularly frustrated, I sometimes headed straight for a shower and then home.

I tried to be as positive as I could after matches and made myself available for photos, especially with kids. But I couldn't always have a smile on my face. A deal to move to Chiangmai FC in late 2023 came at a good time. It meant playing in my mum's home city—my spiritual home in Thailand.

CHAPTER 9
More than just a game

Growing up, David Beckham was a hero for his exploits on the pitch. His right foot was a wand and the source of so many goals for Manchester United, Real Madrid and England. He was also famous for his off-field activities and fashion sense. While I obviously never hit the same heights on the football pitch, I got a flavour of his celebrity and the attention that comes with it.

My first real taste of modelling came when I was at Buriram when we did a Lips magazine shoot with the team. There were photos with the whole squad—one of them saw us all shirtless in the stand. We also had to take some photos with the 'Miss Buriram' of the time and some individual players did shoots on their own. I had to do one sitting in an ice bucket wearing just my underwear.

It felt like a bit of fun as it was something different for me. It was interesting to see how they handled that kind of photo shoot and the kinds of photos they chose to take. It was a reminder of the cultural differences between Thailand and Europe. If I had been forced to take photos in my underwear at a club in Europe, I'm sure I would have taken some stick from my teammates. But it just seemed like no big deal in Thailand.

I did a few more shoots with Buriram, but then the first one I had outside the club was for Chang. It was part of a commercial that the beverage company was making for the 2014 World Cup. The shoot involved some other Buriram players as well as some rival players from other clubs, but again, it was fun to be a part of it.

I really started to be in demand for this kind of work after the 2014 Asian Games. It took off in a big way and I began to do a lot of commercials and magazine shoots.

My first really big contract on my own was with Nivea. I signed a deal to do a series of promotional activities with them just before the 2014 AFF Cup. It was a significant commitment and worth a substantial amount of money, taking me into a different world in terms of earning potential. Nivea was a household name worldwide—the company that sponsored Real Madrid. It was quite something for them to choose me.

The first commercials I shot with them were around February 2015 when I was waiting for my knee surgery. There was a full week of work as I had to shoot three commercials.

While I went there as a football player with a relatively modest career to date, I was treated like a superstar. I had my own bus where I could rest between shoots, and I was provided with great food and even my choice of mineral water brand.

The staff also kept me away from fans so I could stay focused on getting the job done. The Nivea commercial was done just a couple of months after the extraordinary hype of the AFF Cup win, so there was huge interest in my every move. Going through the airport two months previously, I had to wear a cap and sunglasses to avoid being mobbed. My location for the Nivea shoots had been leaked and fans showed up. But I had a job to do, so I couldn't spend a lot of time taking selfies.

It was another reminder of how the previous few months had completely changed my life. But I was just enjoying every moment and didn't really stop to think about what was going on.

It was hard work shooting commercials and it gave me an insight into the world of professional actors and models. I would go to bed at 3am and then get up three hours later to start work on the next shoot. It was a really tough schedule but I couldn't complain given what had been invested in me.

At times like those, I remembered what the Buriram team manager had told me when we were in negotiations over my move to Thailand.

He indicated my off-field potential and he was being proven right. However, I could not have dreamed of one day becoming the face of Nivea in Thailand when I was struggling to break into the first team at Grasshoppers just a few years earlier. I came to Thailand to play football but the opportunity came to me and I embraced it.

I was becoming 'more than an athlete', to borrow from LeBron James. I loved the Nivea tagline 'Game Changer' because I think it was really fitting for the time. Along with several other star players, I was part of a very exciting period in Thai football as more money was invested by sponsors, clubs became more professional and the national team were on a roll.

Another commercial contract I signed was with Nike Singapore. This was a real source of personal pride as it was directly linked to sport and it's such an iconic brand. To be a Nike athlete was always a dream for me as it put me in the company of global superstars like LeBron, Cristiano Ronaldo and Rafael Nadal.

I also signed deals with other brands, including Taro (famous for dried squid snacks), a laundry detergent, FIFA online, and an anti-inflammatory cream. I also did a really cool commercial with BeIN Sports. My best friend from Switzerland was in it, as was the famous Indonesian fan who looked like Ronaldinho. I also advertised Suzuki Swift and was a brand ambassador for Hublot Swiss watches.

All those marketing deals certainly kept me busy and there did come a point when I had to start turning stuff down. I always told myself that the main focus had to be football and I could not let other things get in the way. I was also conscious of how it looked to others. I was worried about what people would say and I did not want to be accused of losing focus on football and thinking I was a superstar.

It's easy for fans and the media to point the finger at someone and suggest that they are more interested in being a celebrity than football. It has happened to players like Beckham and Paul Pogba. It was obviously on a much smaller scale with me, but the principle was the same.

Looking back, I shouldn't have been so sensitive to the opinions of others. I should just have taken all the work I was offered. People will always bitch and be jealous and find something negative to say. So what? I know it's a cliche, but football really is a short career. I had to take advantage while I was such a hot property and make the kind of money that would provide for me and my family in both the short and long term. But while I did plenty of commercial work, I could have done much more and it was probably a mistake to say no sometimes. Now, I always accept offers as long as they fit in with my schedule and the company is one I am happy to work with.

Of course, I have always drawn a line at anything that directly interfered with football. For example, I wasn't going to miss training to attend the launch of a product in a shopping mall. That did mean missing out on opportunities as many big marketing events tended to be held in the early evenings when I was either training or playing.

I was able to attend some marketing events but I never really felt comfortable at them when I was younger. I was a bit of a fish out of water among people who worked in other industries, feeling like I was just a guy who played football. I did start to become more at ease the more I attended as I started to get to know some familiar faces. I also began to recognise the value of networking at these events as they could lead to future opportunities. At first, I felt that I didn't have much in common with the people around me at a product launch but then I started to realise that there were some really interesting people to talk to, so I made the effort.

One event I did attend was to pick up the award for being GQ Man of the Year in 2017. Five years later, I was back at the same event, presenting the same award to Chanathip. After his award ceremony, I was chatting to him and he told me that he could never have imagined standing in front of all the famous people.

He was a kid from a small village in provincial Thailand and we had first met at a very young age as football players only. Now we were being recognised for our contributions to the fashion industry in front of some of Thailand's biggest celebrities and influencers. What a crazy journey it had been.

A byproduct of all of this was interest from some female fans but they never really crossed any lines. While many of them screamed hysterically at matches, when it came to meeting me, they were generally just shy young kids who were sometimes even shaking. It made me feel like a member of a boy band at times. Again, that was a good feeling and a big boost to the ego.

I am aware that my looks are a part of my appeal to brands, so I have to make sure I take care of my appearance. Ever since I was a kid, I have always had a degree of vanity about my appearance. I have always wanted to have a particular style and to look good. It's important for my confidence.

However, it might surprise people that I don't really do anything special. I just do the basics and that's not a lot of work. I use more sunscreen the older I get but the only thing out of the ordinary is that I get a haircut every 10 days. I like to look fresh before a game and I always believed that looking good led to playing well.

Your appearance shows who you are as a person. But it's important to have personal warmth as well as a good fashion sense. No one likes someone who is too arrogant, regardless of the clothes they wear. I also try my best to be approachable and have a smile on my face.

Having a public profile allows you to be a trendsetter and it's nice to see young kids choosing a particular haircut, tattoo or pair of sneakers because of my influence. I know that I am a little bit different from everyone else and that's how I like it.

One of my main indulgences is my fondness for really nice sneakers. I'm a real 'sneakerhead' and lots of young Thai players ask me questions about how or where to buy certain sneakers that are limited editions. Sometimes, I post something about a new pair of sneakers and someone will contact me to ask how to get the same pair. It's flattering.

As a kid in Switzerland, I didn't have many of the pairs of sneakers that I liked because I couldn't afford them. My parents didn't think the more expensive Nike sneakers were worth the money, so I didn't really get into fashion. It seemed like a frivolous use of money to my mum and dad, and I guess I developed the same belief as I had limited cash.

As I got older and started spending more time around professional athletes and at social events, I started to notice more of the fashion trends and developed an interest in them.

I became especially interested in sneakers and started constructing a sneaker wall in my apartment after arriving in Thailand. It really gained momentum after I signed a contract to be a Nike Athlete as it gave me certain privileges. I received lots of pairs of shoes and clothing from them and was also able to get discounts. That's really where my sneaker wall started to gain height!

Of course, I also had enough disposable income to spend some of my money on clothes and shoes from other brands as well as Nike. It was just one of those things that started as an interest and became part of my lifestyle.

Instagram opened my eyes to a lot of the fashion out there and online shopping made it easy to buy whatever I wanted. For a couple of years, I maybe overdid the shopping as I was spending lots of money on special edition sneakers. I had a bit of a scattergun approach and just made a lot of impulse buys and my sneaker wall grew significantly.

But as I got older, I became a bit more focused on the details of the design and the value of the products. There were so many models, so I started to choose more carefully. That was probably just a sign of my taste becoming more refined and also becoming more responsible with money.

My sneaker wall started to get a bit smaller but when I moved from one apartment to another, it was clear that I still had too many pairs. I began the process of reducing my sneaker stock. I gave some pairs away to friends, I sold some of the higher-value pairs online and I donated some to charity auctions.

I was left with the ones I really like. For example, I still love my pairs of the Air Jordan collection. I have Air Jordan 1s, Dunks, Air Max and Air Force. I still have a big sneaker wall but I am now much more selective compared to when buying sneakers seemed to be a minor addiction.

I still monitor the market value of my collection and some of the pairs I bought a couple of years ago have really risen in price. I take good care of all the sneakers I have so if I have to reduce the size of my wall again in the future, at least I should be able to sell them for a decent price.

My wall is more or less a Nike wall and I was reminded of my responsibilities to them on my birthday one year. A friend sent me a nice pair of special edition Asics sneakers as a gift. I posted them on my Instagram story and tagged my friend to thank him. Within 10 minutes, I received a call from Nike and was told to remove the post.

I was a bit surprised. I reminded them that I wasn't wearing the sneakers or recommending them. It was just a thank you message to a friend. But they insisted that the post was inappropriate for me. The conversation was a little heated and I ended it by saying that at least my friend had remembered my birthday. It was perhaps a little petty of me but I thought it had been a little petty of them to contact me so quickly about something that seemed quite trivial.

It had been customary for Nike to send me gifts on my birthday in previous years, and they did eventually respond. A couple of weeks later, they sent me a lovely pair of Air Jordan Off-White sneakers as a way of smoothing things over. I have to say that they are among my favourite pairs. If you check the market now, they are among the rarest and most expensive. The last time I looked, their market value was around US$5,000.

For those that don't really follow the online trade in sneakers, it's important to point out that Nike didn't spend US$5,000 on me. Those sneakers are special editions, so once they sell out, they are no longer for sale at the usual outlets. They can only be bought from online traders and collectors.

Now, I reckon I have about 60–80 pairs at home, but at one point it was about 150. I have my favourites that I wear more often but I am careful to keep them all in good condition.

In addition to sneakers, another of my personal indulgences is tattoos. My older half-sister, Sabrina, has tattoos and I grew up with an interest in them because of her. I always wanted to have at least one tattoo, but, not surprisingly, I wasn't allowed to get any as a kid. However, my dad promised that I could get one if I won the U-17 World Cup. I think he was joking at the time because he wasn't expecting us to go all the way, but he had to keep his promise.

A couple of weeks after I came back from Nigeria as a world champion, we went to a tattoo studio. Because I was still just 17 years old, my dad had to accompany me and give his consent. On my left arm, I had the date of our World Cup final triumph tattooed—15/11/09. That was my first tattoo—paid for by my dad.

That was just the start. There was a story behind the first one and I wanted to continue in that vein. For me, every tattoo has some meaning. Now, my arm has so many tattoos that it looks like things have been put together in a random way, but each individual design has a story behind it.

For example, on my left upper arm there is a Maori/Polynesian-style tattoo. It was inspired by The Rock because, as a big WWE fan, he was one of my heroes. I also have roses. They don't have a specific story, but they are an old-school design that I became familiar with when I was growing up. I saw many people with rose tattoos, and I just wanted to have one.

I also got a tattoo that featured two masks—one with a happy face and the other with a sad face. I got this one after my first injury and the design speaks for itself. We all have good times and bad times, and sometimes we have to smile for the outside world despite feeling sad on the inside. When we experience our toughest moments, we always have to get off the floor and see the light at the end of the tunnel. It is a little bit like the Muhammad Ali quote—"Ain't nothing wrong with going down, it's staying down that's wrong".

I also have family members on my arm and four aces for good luck. On my hand, I have one of my favourites. It features the quote, "Never a failure, always a lesson". I also have my dog, the date of my marriage and several others.

For me, tattooing is an art and I have so much respect for the people who produce that art. It has been interesting to observe how technology has changed the way tattoos are done. When I got my first tattoos, I wanted really thin lines but was told that it wasn't possible because they would fade away over time. However, now technology has made it possible for tattoo artists to do more intricate designs.

There was a time in my mid-20s when I was really into tattoos and a lot of that was related to some of the athletes I looked up to. There was also an influence from my social circles as other people's tattoos gave me ideas.

My tattoos mean a lot to me and, despite the fact that they divide opinion, I never back down from my belief in their aesthetic value. Many years ago, tattoos were associated with the underworld or perhaps people with a rebellious streak. That was especially the case in Thailand as the country has a very conservative side.

However, over time, I believe tattoos have become more accepted in Thai society and that people respect my decision to have them. I remember going to Osaka in Japan when my hair was dyed peroxide blond and I got a lot of looks. I wasn't able to go to any onsens (hot spring baths) because of their ban on tattoos, so it reminded me that this kind of art is not universally accepted.

Fashion and tattoos are important parts of my identity off the pitch, but I can never escape my identity as an athlete. During the football season I'm in Bangkok most of the time, and I still focus on my physical condition when I have a day off. I do extra training because that has been my habit since a very young age. I might do just 30 minutes on the exercise bike but it maintains my routine. I also like going for saunas and steam baths.

Because of my unfortunate experience with injuries, I am very aware of the importance of recovery and I make sure that I stick to the guidance I have been given over the years.

My wife Lena and I don't always have the same days off but when we are both free, we like to watch TV series together, go to the cinema, go out for nice meals or maybe to a spa. My upbringing certainly shaped my taste in films and I have always enjoyed inspirational sports movies, like *Remember the Titans, Coach Carter, Miracle* and the *Rocky* films. *Rocky* was a particular influence in my career as it really helped to motivate me. In addition to sports films, I am also a fan of action movies, war films and crime dramas. My favourite actors are guys like Will Smith and Leonardo DiCaprio.

I guess my situation really forced me to become a film lover because during my first 18 months in Thailand, movies were a very important part of my routine. At Buriram, my life was training, sleeping and watching movies. Away from films, my favourite sitcom is probably *Big Bang Theory* and I finally watched *Game of Thrones* recently—years after everyone else.

Lena is often working on my days off, so I have time to myself and I like to play other sports as well. Of course, I don't have the energy levels that I had in my early 20s so I have to save my energy, but I try to do other things to take my mind off football.

Most of all, I like being around friends. We can talk about things that have nothing to do with my day job, and I can just be myself. As a football player, I have to be conscious of my image as 'Chappuis' but when I am with friends, I can be 'Charyl'. It's a bit like leading a double life, but not in a bad way.

I enjoy talking to friends about my other interests. We talk about music, computer games and food. It's interesting because my life has been so focused on football from an early age that I never really had time to consider some of the finer things in life. Now, I am becoming a bit of a foodie. I am fortunate to live in Thailand where the food is so good. If I had to name the top three countries in the word for food, I would have to say that Italy, Thailand and Japan come out on top.

I'm also more interested in specific drinks. As an athlete, I am obviously careful about my alcohol intake, but I'm also selective with my choice of drinks. As a younger player, when I partied after winning something, I just drank whatever. I didn't think about the brand of vodka or whisky that was going into my glass. In the past, I didn't understand why people spent so much money on alcoholic drinks. For example, I just didn't get why they spent a lot on a specific bottle of wine when much cheaper options were available. But now I understand it. A good wine tastes different, it has a more complex body and it doesn't give you a nasty hangover. As I get older, I am learning more about that kind of thing and it's exciting.

My favourite drink at the moment is a Negroni, but I also love a good glass of red wine with a nice meal. A lot of that influence comes from my Italian friends. Just as they taught me more about how to dress well, they have also opened my eyes to other interesting lifestyle choices. They also give me ideas about what could come after my football career and the kinds of things I might become involved in. It's great to have friends who have a completely different mindset and that come from a community of artists rather than footballers. It's often forgotten that athletes have to make so many sacrifices in terms of the disciplined life we have to follow. When I am with friends from outside the football bubble, I am a little envious of the freedom they have to eat and drink what they want, and to not have to worry so much about getting enough sleep.

Travel is another of my passions. When I have more extended holidays, I love to travel around the world and see and experience new things. I have had many opportunities to travel as part of my career, but I will certainly relish the chance for more leisure travel after I stop playing.

Another thing that I have developed more of an interest in is music and much of that comes from the people I spend time with. My favourite music genres are hip-hop and R&B (rhythm and blues). There was a time when I listened to a lot of reggaeton and was influenced by the multicultural nature of Swiss society. I have also had a lot of teammates from South America, so you hear and start enjoying the music they like in the locker room.

I have some friends who are DJs, so I have started listening to more house and tech house music because of them. I have also developed a better understanding of the art of DJing. In the past, I thought being a DJ was just about pressing the play button but now I know there is much more to it than that. It has definitely broadened my musical horizons. But hip hop and R&B remain my number one styles of music. I like Drake and The Weekend in particular.

In terms of other sports, I really got into the NBA and NFL when I moved to Thailand. That was mainly because the time difference makes watching

American sports so much easier than European football. In Thailand, we train and play in the evening, so in the mornings, we are free to watch sport and the timing often coincides with live basketball and American football matches. With YouTube and social media, there is so much additional coverage, so I developed a keen interest.

You have to admire NFL players. They are proper athletes—real monsters. I look up to them for the way they train and the background stories they have. Many of them came from nothing and sport kept them alive and off the streets. Watching these guys compete at the highest level just adds to my personal motivation.

I grew up watching so many sports but basketball and American football came later. I have become a big fan of the Golden State Warriors because of Stephen Curry and the fact that their golden era really began just after I arrived in Thailand.

It's a strange thing to say but I don't watch that much football anymore. In Switzerland, it was a midweek tradition to stay at home and watch the Champions League games on TV. With the time difference now, it's almost impossible to watch the matches live. In exceptional cases, I might make a point of seeing them but usually it's just highlights on YouTube.

I watch other Thai League matches and English Premier League games at the weekend. But I always make sure to catch up with the Barcelona games and the German Bundesliga. I have a stronger attachment to the Bundesliga than the EPL as it was something that I grew up with. I have only started watching more EPL matches in Thailand because it is by far the most popular league in the country.

I like Bayern Munich and Borussia Dortmund and I am a huge fan of Freiburg because they have punched above their weight so often. I have always kept an eye on Hamburg because I came close to joining them. In the EPL, I mainly follow Arsenal because Xhaka, who was once a teammate, played there for so long and because they play beautiful football.

I don't know why but I don't really pay much attention to Swiss football anymore. That may be because of the frustration I felt when I was trying to make the breakthrough with Grasshoppers. I had very positive experiences when I went on loan but the Swiss Super League reminds me of a difficult period in my life and perhaps that's why I have generally lost interest in it. I check in on Grasshoppers now and then, but I don't really follow it closely.

Despite growing up in Switzerland, Barcelona has always been the club closest to my heart. As a kid, I remember the titanic battles they had against Chelsea in the Champions League and some amazing matches against Real Madrid.

But, despite my life revolving around football since the age of five, I have to admit that I am more drawn to other sports now. The passion that I had for Barcelona as a child is what I feel now for Golden State. Even when I'm back in Europe, I get up in the middle of the night for their games.

One of my other great loves is dogs. I had one when I was child but we had to give it away when we moved from a house to an apartment complex where dogs were not allowed. Since that time, I have been an animal lover but I have always been more into dogs because I am allergic to cats.

We had a Chow Chow that unfortunately passed away at a young age but we have since taken on another one. I had never heard of that breed previously. I was more into Pit Bulls before but Lena introduced me to Chow Chows and we now have Nara, who is four years old.

It's great to come home after a hard training session and be greeted by our dog showing love and emotion. Bangkok is not the most dog-friendly city but we have worked out a good walking route every morning and evening.

It has been such a great journey to make this life for myself in a new country and to make so many new friends, meet my wife and develop so many new interests. Sometimes, I think back to my life at Buriram at 21 years old. It might have been very rewarding professionally if I had stayed longer. But the strict routine may have prevented me from having the life experiences that I value so much. I certainly have no regrets about the way things have turned out.

CHAPTER 10
Life after playing

The clock never stops ticking and retirement eventually comes into the view of every player. For some, it is a dark moment that creates great anxiety. Ever since it started to concern me, I have been determined to be as well prepared as possible for the day my legs give up on me.

In my early twenties, retirement never really crossed my mind. In my first couple of years in Thailand, I didn't give any thought to what would happen after my playing career came to an end. Coming from Switzerland, I was always taught to be prepared for life after football and I had to finish my schooling and my parents constantly reminded me not to neglect my studies.

But I only really started to think about life after football when Lena began to push me to give it more serious thought. It was the push that I needed to start preparing.

Of course, I can't really properly discuss my future without looking back at how I met the person who has helped me to shape it. In 2017, I broke up with my previous girlfriend and, for the first time in my adult life, I suddenly found myself single. We had been together since just after I won the U-17 World Cup with Switzerland, so it was sad, but one of those things that happens in life.

This is not meant to sound unkind, but ending that relationship was somewhat of a relief. I had just signed for Muangthong United and it felt like a new beginning for me in many ways. I was 25 years old, single, living in Bangkok and playing for the champions of Thailand. I decided to cut loose a little and I swapped my Toyota Yaris for an Audi TP. I tuned my new car and started driving around with a little more swagger—the classic look of the single young footballer. It was fortunate that my dad wasn't around to kick my ass and bring me back down to earth. At the same time, it was a stage of life that helped shape me as I made a few mistakes that I learned from. I'm not proud of some of my behaviour, but I don't regret it because they were all valuable experiences.

It's not an excuse, but I think my behaviour had a lot to do with the fact that I had just ended such a long relationship that felt stifling at times. I couldn't go anywhere or do anything without letting my ex-girlfriend know. I found myself sometimes lying because I wanted to go somewhere with friends and maybe told her that I had some football-related business to deal with. It's obviously unhealthy when that starts to happen.

We were so young when our relationship started and we had some great times, but there were some very significant issues towards the end. I didn't want to lie and I didn't want to be controlled. When you are controlled, you cannot be yourself and, to be yourself, you end up lying.

Of course, it was difficult for my ex-girlfriend to deal with the sudden fame I was experiencing from back in Switzerland. We had been trying to make a long-distance relationship work before she moved to Thailand in 2015. Sadly, it just didn't work out. She wanted to live in Bangkok while I was playing in Suphanburi. That meant I was constantly travelling between Suphanburi and Bangkok, which was exhausting.

She had given up her life in Switzerland to be with me, but the reality was very difficult as I was so busy and she didn't really have much to do apart from wait for me to be able to spend time with her. I tried my best to make it work by looking into ways she could get more settled by studying or developing and sticking to some kind of routine. But in the end, it just felt like I was always under pressure to get home as soon as possible to maximise my time with her. I wasn't free to spontaneously go for dinner with friends whenever I wanted, or I had to plan it weeks in advance so I could break the news to her.

It became very clear that we had grown apart. I had gone from being an aspiring professional footballer in Switzerland when we met to being a famous footballer in a completely different culture, with a high profile off the field as well. No matter how much you want to make a relationship work, when you realise you are not happy anymore, you have to make a very difficult decision. We decided to call it a day, which was difficult after eight years. There were obviously many good moments in that time, but our lifestyles and some of our priorities had completely changed.

My newfound freedom meant I started to go out a lot and it was on one of those nights out that I met my future wife in a nightclub. It may sound a little cheesy but I knew from day one that she was the right one for me. I was out with a group of my friends and she was with her best friend Jennifer and we just got talking. I actually connected with Jennifer at first and Lena was still in a long-term relationship of her own.

Nevertheless, despite the obstacles, it seemed that I had caught Lena's eye and, for me, it was important to build trust with her friend. Over time, we met more often, sometimes randomly. Although Bangkok is a huge city, certain social groups tend to frequent the same places, so we bumped into each other quite regularly.

The breakthrough came when I sent an emoji of a tomato in response to a story she had posted on Instagram. She replied and suggested that I could communicate more effectively by asking how she was and actually making conversation. That was when we started talking more and it turned out that she wasn't happy in her relationship and was planning to end it. I had already started falling for her, so that was very interesting news for me. It meant that I had a chance.

We started dating in the usual way —going for meals and trips to the cinema. She was a bit unsure if it would be a serious thing, so I had to work hard to convince her. Because I had been having fun as a single man for the previous few months, perhaps I had earned a bit of a reputation as someone who just wanted a bit of a good time without any commitments. Her friends were certainly warning her that she should be careful with me, given my profile and recent behaviour.

But I persisted and managed to convince her that I was serious. Just before I returned to Switzerland to visit my family for Christmas, our relationship began to get serious. During my trip home, we spoke for a long time every day despite the time difference. I even changed my return flight so that I could get back to Thailand a little earlier just to be with her.

We had to keep the relationship quiet to begin with as Lena was working for an agency that had strict rules about their employees' public image. When they are trying to help someone become a TV or movie star, they don't want the public to know they have a partner. That's especially important on social media as the belief is that appearing to be single heightens your appeal for fans.

However, we couldn't hide our relationship forever. After she came to watch me in an ACL qualifier, the rumours started and the truth eventually came out. It was no secret from then on, and we started to attract more attention on social media. I had become so used to having a focus on me that I didn't really notice when photos were taken of us. However, it was a new thing for Lena, so it took a bit of getting used to.

It wasn't long before we more or less moved in together. We did still have our own places, and that felt important to me as I tried to avoid repeating the mistakes of my previous relationship. I like to be able to have my own space and have time to myself, and Lena seemed to feel the same way. It has always felt like finding my soulmate. She gives me the space that I was looking for. She works hard and travels a lot and it's the same for me. We are apart quite a lot because of our jobs, but that just makes our time together more precious.

Our connection maybe had much to do with us having similar backgrounds. Like me, her parents separated when she was a child and she mostly grew up with her dad. Her connection to Thailand also comes from her mother's side and she also arrived in Thailand to pursue a dream. From day one, I could see the fire in her to be successful so she could take care of her family, and that made a strong impression on me.

Even now, she never slows down. She has made a success of her career as a model and businesswoman but she is always looking for the next challenge. I was also impressed by her ability to brush off the fact that she didn't really make it as an actor. She was very philosophical about the situation and, ultimately, she is happy to be out of that scene because it can be quite restrictive. Now, she has the freedom to post what she likes on social media and do whatever she wants.

Lena has her own clothing brands and she is her own boss at a relatively young age. I still have a somewhat old-fashioned attitude and feel that I should provide for her. She appreciates that but she is very strong and can take care of herself.

We actually got engaged quite soon after we started dating and we wanted to get married earlier than we did but COVID got in the way before we ultimately had our dream wedding in Tuscany in June 2022.

It was quite a small wedding but, as our careers both require us to keep up our social media profiles, we made sure there was plenty of video footage and photos to share. We had done some vlogs together to share details of our everyday lives, so it didn't really feel like an invasion of privacy. Vogue Magazine's Thailand edition published the photos and that widened our audience significantly.

Part of the reason for sharing them was that so few people attended the wedding. In Thailand, weddings can be very big, lavish affairs but we wanted ours to be more intimate and in an idyllic setting that appealed to both of us. Having the photos published meant that fans and our wider groups of friends could see how it went.

It surprised some people that there were so few teammates at our wedding, but that was just a reflection on how things were at the time. I wasn't really involved much at Port and did not feel part of things, so only Antony Ampapitakwong and Top made it from the football world. Unfortunately, Chitchanok couldn't come as he was recovering from surgery.

As I keep saying, it's important for me to do things my way. Our preference for a wedding abroad with only close friends and family may have upset a few people, but that's their problem.

Lena and I are not under any illusions that we're big superstars, but we're aware that we attract more publicity as a couple than we do individually. Instagram posts that feature both of us always get more engagement than posts of either of us alone. As a businesswoman, Lena understands more than me about how to generate social media engagement and how to connect with fans. That's a positive thing in our lives. We still need a degree of privacy as well, so we are careful about what we post, but we both understand the need to maintain a high profile to maximise our opportunities.

Lena's perspective is interesting because she came into my life after I had become a big name in Thailand but also after the hype around me had subsided somewhat. She never knew me when I was experiencing my biggest highs, but she has always supported me and helped me through the frustrating times. From my side, there is still motivation to prove to her and to myself that I still have something to offer as a player, so she pushes me to improve in all aspects of life.

She had never really been a football fan, so it was a completely new thing for her to understand the life of an athlete because she has had a very different journey. She studied for a long time, then became a model and is now a businesswoman who has a lot of things going on. She works really hard and that is reflected in how she pushes me to get started on my post-career plans. I have huge respect for what she has achieved through her own hard work and that motivates me to do more.

For the past couple of years, I have started looking into opportunities and thinking about what might suit me beyond my playing days. It would be nice to build the foundations for something now, so there is a smooth transition rather than a completely fresh start. At the ages of 28 and 29, I started to look ahead. That timing was also partly because it was when I fell out of favour at my club and it changed my mindset.

It was difficult for me to accept that I was no longer a first-choice player after spending so many years playing a key role in a variety of teams.

However, it also gave me a reminder that a football career comes to an end sooner rather than later. Approaching 30 years old, I was entering the final stages. Being given less time on the pitch forced me to think more about what I had to offer off the pitch. I reflected on my abilities and my strengths and weaknesses to try and figure out what I might be good at.

I thought back to the times when I had to turn down commercial opportunities to focus on my football. Now, it feels like it's time to look out for myself more. It is a cliche, but the career of an athlete is short and uncertain. Some of us can make very good money, especially for people of our age group, but we have to save for the future and invest wisely in case things become difficult when we have to retire.

It's not easy when it dawns on you that you have just three or four years left to play. It's true that nowadays, science is allowing athletes to have longer careers at the top. To have Lionel Messi, Cristiano Ronaldo, Robert Lewandowski, Luka Modric and Karim Benzema among the best in the world in their mid-30s is amazing and shows just what is possible with the right lifestyle, support and a bit of luck.

In Thailand, it can be possible to extend your career with the right club owner behind you or if you're willing to drop down a level. But I'm not sure that appeals to me, especially after all the injury troubles I have had. Waking up after a 90-minute match can be painful and you start to ask yourself if you really want to go through another pre-season.

My goal is to play until my mid-30s and end my career on a high but what happens off the pitch is equally important. Like most people, I want to start a family, so that is just as much of a focus as work.

I'm lucky to have been able to see many sides of life. I have friends who are famous actors, models and artists and they have opened me to other ways of living and thinking. My circle of friends is also very multinational, and many are half-Thai like me. There is also a range of ages from early 20s to mid-30s. This diversity has had a big impact and it's also a group of ambitious people, so we push each other to achieve more. I see that as a very healthy thing. It's not competition that can lead to jealousy but a support network that wants the best for everyone.

I'm lucky to have these kinds of friends because they prevent me from becoming complacent and motivate me to look ahead and not back. It would be easy for me to live off my past and spend time talking about how I was once a world champion and a treble winner, etc. Those are great memories that will always be cherished but they are in the past and I hopefully have a long life ahead of me where I will achieve more and create new memories.

Of course, I have also been very lucky to have such supportive parents throughout my career to date and they will continue to have my back and give sound advice for my future goals. And then there are the other people who have been there for me through both the good times and bad. My agent has been such a dependable presence and I have a team of people who I can trust to look out for my best interests. Not everyone is lucky enough to be surrounded by such a strong support group so I never take that for granted. Together, we are all going to be well prepared for what happens at the end of my playing career.

Of course, it's impossible to know exactly how it will feel to stop playing. There are worries and there is some anxiety, but that's normal. The last 10 years in Thailand have been unbelievable, way beyond what I could reasonably have expected when I signed for Buriram at the age of 21. Obviously, those 10 years have packed in so much and enriched my life in ways I could never have imagined. My football career has had its ups and downs, but off the pitch there have been so many new experiences that have given so much meaning to my life.

I have some friends who have already retired and some admit they miss the camaraderie that football gives. A football team is a second family for a lot of people and leaves a big emotional gap when it's gone. However, while I generally enjoy being part of the group, I don't see myself missing it that much. I am going to miss playing and working hard to achieve something and win trophies, but I have always had a social life outside football.

Despite some concerns, I truly believe that what comes next will be positive and a lot of that confidence is down to the people around me.

It's important to focus on the plus side and my wife will be happy that I will have a bit more control over my schedule and that there will be fewer surprises to deal with. It will be nice to be able to plan holidays in advance rather than having to book things at the last minute when a window opens up because we have been knocked out of a cup competition.

I'm also looking forward to being my own boss and not always having to be somewhere at a certain time because that's what someone else decides. It will be nice to have more control over my life than I have had as a professional footballer. For example, it will be nice to be a little more relaxed about accepting another glass of wine or another slice of pizza. But I will never let myself go in terms of my diet and appearance. I have been programmed to take good care of myself for so long and that's something I can't see changing.

The transition may be easier because of the way my career has gone. When you're no longer a first-team regular, you gradually lose a bit of the edge you used to have. That's also because of age and reassessing your priorities. In the past, if a friend was having a birthday party in the evening, I just wouldn't go because it might affect my sleeping patterns or some other aspect of my routine. Now, I am much more inclined to say yes to social invitations because I place more value on my personal relationships.

Those personal relationships are a big part of the reason why, despite spending the first 20 years of my life in Switzerland, I see my future in Thailand. It's a beautiful country and Lena and I are forever connected to it by family ties. The opportunities we have here make it more logical for us to be based here. We are lucky that our other countries are as nice as Sweden and Switzerland and we can always go back there for holidays to visit friends and family. I hope to have more time for travelling in the future and that will mean more trips back to Switzerland and other European countries.

I do miss certain aspects of life in Europe. Of course, I miss my family and friends but on a recent visit I realised that I really miss long summer days. Because the Thai football calendar used to run from about February to October, I didn't have the opportunity to go back to Europe in the summer months after coming to Thailand. With the change of the schedule in 2021, I finally had the chance to have a summer holiday in Europe in 2022. I had almost forgotten that the sun doesn't set until around 10 or 10.30pm in June and July. I miss that feeling of being outside with friends having a barbecue as the light fades gradually over the evening. In Thailand, it gets dark between 6 and 7pm all year round, so it's a huge contrast.

In terms of my specific goals for the future, I have thought about several things. Coaching can be a popular and logical move for many former players. It doesn't require a complete upheaval in your way of life but, to be a successful head coach, it does mean you have to work much harder than you ever did as a player. To be honest, it has never held much appeal to me. I love sports and the life of an athlete—it's who I am. I have been through years of trying to keep myself motivated and taking care of myself to ensure I am giving my best performances when I play. But maybe I have just seen too much of what a head coach's life involves. I'm really not sure that I would want to live that life.

But you never know. At the moment, it's difficult to imagine myself taking that role but things can change and if I miss the action, I could be tempted. However, it seems unlikely right now.

Working in the media is another popular option for ex-players but, again, it's not something that I have thought much about. That may be partly due to the fact that any work would likely require me to speak in my second or third languages (i.e., English or Thai), and that would be challenging. It doesn't mean that I have no interest in doing it, but it's not something I have been considering as an option. If someone approached me and asked me to be a studio guest or a co-commentator, I would certainly give it some thought but unless that happens, I'm unlikely to be seeking these kinds of opportunities.

For now, I have different targets and I see myself as much more suited to identifying talent and developing it at an early age. I find it fascinating how people watch the same games and the same players but can have completely different interpretations. That's what attracts me to scouting for players.

It's a real challenge to spot teenagers with the right skill set and temperament to have a career in the game, but it's something that really appeals to me.

I generally enjoy watching youth academy games more than professional games. No disrespect to my Thai League rivals, but I would sooner watch an academy match between U16 or U-17 teams than a game between, for example, Prachuap and Sukhothai. For me, it's more interesting to see young talents and that's the direction I see myself moving in. With my connections to Europe and the name I have made for myself, not just in Thailand but also in Southeast Asia, I really think I can help young kids to improve. With my experience, I would love to support them and ultimately provide pathways for Thai players to play in Europe.

At the moment, young players are too connected to one club in Thai football. In Europe, it is not like that. If a youth team player from Zurich wants to go to a different club in Europe, the transfer would go through their agent or representative and not through the club president, which is often the practice here. It won't be possible to change this situation overnight, but in the future it's important that agents work with club presidents to ensure the focus is on what's best for the long-term career of the player rather than the short-term plan for the club.

It will take time and patience to convince players and those connected to them that the process of becoming a top player is gradual and that's where the challenges lie.

I would love to have a player agency in Thailand. I am already working towards this and educating myself on what's involved in preparation for the end of my playing days. I can offer help in terms of identifying the key add-ons for players to rise above the competition. That might be extra training on specific aspects of their game and it might be helping with the psychological elements, dietary advice or building physical strength—whatever gives them the edge. I would really like to bring elements of the American athlete's lifestyle to Asia.

My initial idea for my agency would be to work with a small group of core players and give them very specialised support. I wouldn't want 100 players on my books. I would like to have someone always available to help my players and if that means taking phone calls in the middle of the night from a player who is homesick in Europe, then that's fine. To succeed, it would need that level of dedication.

I would want the players working with me to have the same kinds of opportunities that I had as a kid and that would mean creating a very strong support group to deal with all of the challenges young players face.

I still have so much to learn about being an agent, but using my own experiences seems a good place to start. There is so much potential in Thailand but it seems that young players are not getting the right opportunities. This is a country of almost 70 million people and football is the most popular sport. It doesn't seem right that we have never produced players who have got anywhere near the top level of the game. It's something that I want to help put right.

If Thailand ever wants to reach a World Cup, we have to look at what other countries are doing and learn from them. For example, players might need to leave home a little earlier to develop their talents because at 22 or 23, it may already be too late. There are so many steps in the process, including learning a new language.

For me, it seems that kids should be looking to go abroad between the ages of 16 and 18. At the very least, they might get the opportunity to train with better players, see different training methods and build their physical strength. If they decide to return to Thailand, that's fine, but they will have benefited from the experience and they may have developed a stronger mindset.

We should always be looking at Japan as an example. Kazu Miura went to Brazil at the age of 15 to try and make it in the professional game. He may not have made a huge impact there but after returning home, he became arguably Japan's first football superstar and holds legendary status both there and across Asia for his legacy. Even at the peak of his powers, he still wanted the opportunity to improve, leading him to go to Italy and play for Genoa at the age of 27. Again, his impact there was limited, but it was more evidence of his determination to play at the highest level.

When Kazu was starting out, Japan had never qualified for a World Cup. He played a key role in their first ever successful qualifying campaign as they finally reached the finals of the 1998 tournament in France. Another key member of that qualifying campaign was Hidetoshi Nakata, a player who left for Perugia after that World Cup when he was just 21 years old. He would go on to have a more successful time in Italy than Kazu, playing for several top sides and winning Serie A with Roma in 2001.

Those two players were pioneers and Japan now qualify for every World Cup and produce top talents who play in the best leagues in Europe. Thailand should be looking to emulate that but it will take time and a lot of effort.

In addition to my plans to establish an agency for young Thai players, I have firm plans to open an academy. These plans were developed with the company I am working with—Capital Performance.

Again, my upbringing helps my vision for the academy. I was always training and playing from a very young age. I went to a sports school and received an education that enabled me to focus on football, and I was constantly being pushed by those around me. I want young Thai players to have these kinds of opportunities and let's see where it can take them. I genuinely believe an academy would work well in Thailand and, who knows, perhaps there could ultimately be hubs across Southeast Asia in countries like Indonesia, Malaysia and Singapore. They are exciting ideas but, for now, they are just ideas. I really hope my team and I can make them happen in the coming years.

I'm well aware of the potential barriers and the challenges to overcome. At the moment, most Thai players come from very modest backgrounds and sometimes poverty. Football is a great way out for them and it's also very rewarding for them to have the opportunity to support their families. They can sometimes quickly go from earning next to nothing to making what is a very decent salary in Thailand. The problem is that escalation can make players too comfortable and less ambitious. They reach a plateau and become averse to taking risks because they don't want to put their lifestyle in jeopardy.

We have to be very conscious of the fact that lots of youngsters have the hunger to keep improving until they sign their first big contract. Suddenly, they can go from eating instant noodles to eating the best food at nice restaurants. They can also treat their parents and other family members, and that's obviously something they don't want to give up. That's where I see myself coming in. I could advise on the next step and reassure them that it makes sense to take risks to reach their full potential.

A lot of the groundwork will involve building trust with parents. My ten years of playing in Thailand and being successful with the national side will really help with that. I have a name that is recognised and that should not be underestimated. It's very difficult for agents to get started, especially in a foreign country, but I have established a reputation that should help to make things easier. It should also help me to build trust with any foreign agents that I bring in to help.

I know that agents can sometimes have an image problem and, from the outside, they are sometimes perceived to be people who are looking after their own financial interests rather than the best interests of the players they represent. I hope my background as a player will help me to convince players that I want what's best for them rather than what's best for me. I know exactly what it's like to be 17 years old and have agents asking to represent me and making promises. It's very difficult to know who to trust.

I also know what it feels like to suffer a serious injury and have an agent who doesn't abandon you. I would want my players to know that, even if things go wrong, there will be support for them.

Without wanting to sound arrogant, there are no other agents currently working in Thailand who have had a playing career with as much success as me. Some of them have played at a decent level, but they have never had the same profile as me. That's something I intend to take advantage of. It's similar to brand recognition in shopping. We often buy products at higher prices because we trust the brand to deliver consistent quality.

I would like to use the brand I have built over the past decade to convince players that they should work with me.

It will then be up to me to demonstrate that I deserve their trust and the faith they put in me, and I am confident I will be able to do that. I'm lucky that the agent I have worked with since I was 19 years old is a lawyer. As well as taking care of my contracts very well, he already makes a good living for himself, so it never feels like he's desperate for more money.

While my future focus is mainly on my agency and academy, I also have an eye on something completely different—a bit of acting. I have already had a few offers that I have had to refuse because acting just hasn't been possible to fit acting into my schedule. I hope to get another chance as it's something I would love to try. I don't know if I would be any good at it, but acting appeals to me. Eric Cantona and Vinnie Jones have managed to make a success of it after football, so why not?

I have actually had an offer to play a character based on myself in a Thai series. It's funny because the storyline fits the later stages of my career when I have found it more difficult to exert the influence I once had. Like most of these kinds of series, it would be a love story and I would like to give it a shot. The script would have me in a supporting role, which is ideal as I certainly wouldn't want to be the star given my lack of experience. The director of the series is a big name and it could lead to more work if I do well.

However, while I remain a football player, I can only do acting if it fits my schedule. A couple of years ago, I would just have said no without any hesitation. Now, I'm at a different stage in life and need to give more careful consideration to offers like it as they could open a door that leads to much more than one bit-part role in one series.

Acting is something I had never really thought about before, so it just goes to show that my brand remains strong even if the peak of my football career has passed. As a novice, I still have no idea how hard it would be and how much time I would need to practise and commit to a project. Playing myself should obviously make things easier than being asked to play an unfamiliar role, but I'm sure that it would be a steep learning curve. People train for years to be actors so I know it wouldn't be easy.

Another possibility is to have my own clothing line. I have looked into that and had talks about it with various parties, but it hasn't happened yet. It's still something that I am keen to do but I won't do it half-heartedly. Because of the way I am, anything I do needs to be done properly and to certain standards. That hasn't been possible yet with a potential clothing line, so I'll wait until the time is right and I have the right team in place.

It's not easy to have a successful clothing line and I'm not going to try it just for the sake of having one. My wife already has her own brand but it took several years of hard work for it to take off. I am well aware of the challenges involved in the fashion industry so it's important to get things right. Like with acting, I would be a beginner when it comes to trying to create my own clothing line, so I would need a partner I could trust and learn from before making it happen. My partner would also have to be someone who can take on the bulk of the work, allowing me to focus on football-related work and eventually other things as well.

I know friends who have launched their own clothing lines to varying degrees of success, and their experiences help to educate me on what's required to be successful. I'm in no rush to do it. If it happens, that would be great, but it's not something that's especially important to me.

My post-playing interests won't all be about work, of course. I'm pretty sure I'll continue to play sports regularly after I retire from football, though I'm not sure how intense I'll be and how far I'll want to go. I know some football players really get into other sports after retirement and become really good at them. For example, Bixente Lizarazu won the World Cup and European Championships with France and the Champions League with Bayern Munich, and then became a European jiu-jitsu champion after he retired. There is speculation that there might be a career in golf for Gareth Bale because he has reached such a high level. But I don't really see myself putting in enough time and effort to hit those heights.

I do want to improve at golf but I just don't have enough time to practise.

One of my sporting heroes, Steph Curry, is apparently a great golfer but he has been playing since he was a kid so I'm definitely a long way behind. I would love to ski regularly again but I'm obviously in the wrong country for that. I'm getting into padel tennis and it's gaining a lot of popularity in Europe. In Thailand, it has started to develop and it's great fun to play with friends. Pickleball is another growing sport that I have an interest in. Sport has always been my life and there is no way I can see myself losing the discipline of getting regular exercise and staying in shape.

Looking further ahead, ten years from now, I would love, first of all, to have a happy and healthy family. I also want to have control over my time. I want to be able to decide when I get up in the morning and not always be under pressure to get things done. I hope that my projects are successful and that some of my investments are doing well.

If my agency is going well, I hope it's a sustainable business that doesn't require too much input from me personally. Of course, I will still be heavily involved but I want to have a team who takes care of the day-to-day operations and allows me to be more selective about what my roles are. Most of all, I hope we aren't under such financial pressure that we have to make decisions to cut costs rather than giving the best service we can. That will be difficult but it has to be the aim.

As I mentioned, my agent never pushed me to do something I didn't want to do because he needed money. I want to be in a similar position—making the best decisions rather than decisions that are informed by money alone.

The financial side of things is very important to me because I'm well aware of the problems some former players have. It's sad when footballers make enough money during their careers to set themselves up for a comfortable retirement but then get involved in the wrong projects and become bankrupt. I certainly want to ensure that I am comfortable financially.

I am generally very cautious when it comes to investment so that protects me to some extent, though it also means I miss out on opportunities.

For example, in 2016, a friend of a friend advised me to invest in Bitcoin. Even though he was only suggesting a $1,000 investment, it didn't make sense to me, so I didn't invest, but that's a part of learning. I have also made investments where the stock has gone down in value but again, that's part of the game.

The person I count on most for my financial advice is my agent. I always ask for his opinions when it comes to investing in stock or pitching a business idea. He has advised me on my company, Capital Performance, and another project I'm involved in called *Yes We Trust*, which is an App. Of course, there are no guarantees of success, so you just have to put your faith in other people's knowledge and experience.

While a happy family life and financial security are my priorities, achieving the right balance between professional projects and personal interests will be important. I will have fond memories of my playing career, but life after it holds so much promise.

APPENDIX 1
Charyl Chappuis Honours

Switzerland U-17
2017 World Cup winner

Thailand U23
2013 SEA Games gold medal
2014 Asian Games—4th place

Thailand
2014 AFF Cup winner
2016 AFF Cup winner

Buriram United
2013 Thai League 1 winner
2013 Thai League Cup winner
2013 Thai FA Cup winner

Muangthong United
2017 Thai League Cup winner

APPENDIX 2
My best XIs

Best International XI I have played with (4-3-3)

Benjamin Siegrist
(Switzerland U-17)

Narubadin Weerawatnodom (Thailand NT) — **Osmar Ibanez** (Buriram United) — **Frederic Veseli** (Switzerland U-17) — **Ricardo Rodriguez** (Switzerland U-17)

Charyl Chappuis — **Granit Xhaka** (Switzerland U-17) — **Theerathon Bunmathan** (Buriram United and Thailand NT)

Bjorn Lindemann (Suphanburi) — **Nassim Ben Khalifa** (Switzerland U-17) — **Heberty Fernandes** (Muangthong United)

Best Thai XI I have played with (4-3-3)

Siwarak Tedsungnoen
(Buriram United)

Anawin Jujeen (Buriram United) — **Pratum Chuthong** (Suphanburi) — **Tanaboon Kesarat** (Muangthong United) — **Theerathon Bunmathan** (Buriram United)

Charyl Chappuis — **Sarach Yooyen** (Muangthong United) — **Chanathip Songkrasin** (Thailand NT)

Adisak Kraisorn (Muangthong United) — **Teerasil Dangda** (Muangthong United) — **Kroekrit Thaweekarn** (Thailand NT)

Best XI players I have played against (4-3-3)

Alisson Becker
(Brazil U-17)

Dani Alves (Barcelona) — **Gerard Pique** (Barcelona) — **Shkodran Mustafi** (Germany U-17) — **Adriano** (Barcelona)

Cesc Fabregas (Barcelona) — **Casemiro** (Brazil U-17) — **Mario Gotze** (Germany U-17)

Philippe Coutinho (Brazil U-17 and Liverpool) — **Neymar** (Brazil U-17 and Barcelona) — **Lionel Messi** (Barcelona)

Acknowledgements

So many people have helped me on my journey as a player and a person.

I want to thank all of the teammates who have helped me in my development over the years - all the way from childhood to the present.

I want to thank all of the coaches who have played their part in the good times and in helping me through the difficult years. A special mention goes to Dany Ryser whose faith in me made me a world champion. I also want to thank Davide Morandi, whose trust helped me enjoy football again.

I am forever grateful to Kiatisuk Senamuang (Zico) for making me a Thailand international player and for showing trust in me after my injury troubles. I also appreciate how Velizar Popov brought out the best in me at Suphanburi.

Rolf Muller has been a loyal friend and, as my agent, has provided invaluable advice and assistance for many years.

To my fans - your support through the good times and bad times has been so special and so important. I am really grateful for your loyalty.

There are far too many friends to mention but I love you all and I appreciate all that you do for me. I have to thank my mum and dad and the rest of my family for all of their love and support and for keeping me grounded.

And, finally, thanks to my wonderful wife Lena who has been by my side through some uncertain years and whose love has kept me going.

Special thanks to Vachira Kalong (Almonfoto) and Chiraphat Phaungmala (@supersub Thailand) for their excellent photos.

Charyl Chappuis

About the Authors

Charyl Chappuis is a Swiss-Thai footballer whose career has seen him win several honours at domestic and international level for Thailand.

Paul Murphy is an independent football writer based in Bangkok. He has covered Asian football for over a decade, with a primary focus on Thai football.

MORE REALLY GOOD BOOKS FROM FAIR PLAY PUBLISHING

Noddy, The Untold Story of Adrian Alston

Tales of South American Football

"Get Your Tits Out for the Lads"

George Best Down Under

Football Fans In Their Own Write...

Hear Us Roar – An anthology of emerging women football writers

The First Matildas The 1975 Asian Ladies Championship

Michelle Ford Olympic Champion Turning the Tide

Available from
fairplaypublishing.com.au/shop
and all good bookstores

www.ingramcontent.com/pod-product-compliance
Lightning Source LLC
Chambersburg PA
CBHW041144110526
44590CB00027B/4119